NIGHT OWL PRAYERS

A PRAYERBOOK

ROBERT W. LEE

Also by *Robert W. Lee*

Stained-Glass Millennials

A Sin by Any Other Name
Reckoning with Racism and the Heritage of the South

The Pulpit and the Paper
A Pastor's Coming of Age in Newsprint

Fostering Hope
A Prayerbook for Foster and Adoptive Families

To Barbara Lee, my Nana

I fully believe I received some of my sleeping habits from you. Nonetheless, your presence in my life has been the greatest gift a grandson could hope for. I hope you feel the fullness of my gratitude today and always.

I want to walk as a child of the light.
I want to follow Jesus.
God set the stars to give light to the world.
The star of my life is Jesus.

In him there is no darkness at all.
The night and the day are both alike.
The Lamb is the light of the city of God.
Shine in my heart, Lord Jesus.

—Kathleen Thompson
Excerpt from "I Want to Walk as
a Child of the Light"

ACKNOWLEDGMENTS

The acknowledgments section of a book is such a fickle friend. I have learned to be careful whom I acknowledge, as they are forever tied to my work. I want this book to last as long as it can, so the people listed here have proven their generous willingness not to give up on me. Perhaps this small token of my appreciation might begin to repay all the debts I owe them for their kindness, relationships, and compassion.

First, this book is dedicated to Barbara Lee, my paternal grandmother—my Nana. When I was younger, I would spend the night at her house, and we would both have trouble sleeping. We'd end up watching episodes of *The Golden Girls* or *Antiques Roadshow*. Nana has always had trouble sleeping, and perhaps I received such a gift from her that I might also have that problem. Despite that less-than-ideal gift, her other gifts to the world, to our family, and to me are numerous and exorbitant. The world does not yet fully realize the fullness of generosity and love that she has shown countless people. I count it a big deal to be Nana's grandson. She is married to Bob, my Granddaddy. He is a poet and a renaissance man. I am grateful for them both.

To Stephanie, my love and stay this past decade: Thank you for bearing with me all these nights you've had to hold down the fort while I worked at the hotel and scribbled down these prayers. I was thinking of you the entire time. You are grace to me. Thank you for the ways you show up for our family and have made me a better person, parent, and pastor.

To Athena: Sweet girl, you are a budding theologian even if you never darken the door of a seminary. You have asked me more thoughtful questions about God and life than I've found on seminary exams. Don't ever forget that you are enough and complete simply because you are a child of God, and you are a child of mine.

To Phoenix: My chaotic five-year-old, how lucky I am to see you learn to pray. Don't ever stop learning. Keep trying to be your best self because it is beautiful. You are fearfully and wonderfully made. As you love the animals around you, so too does God love you.

To Sherrie: Thank you for the ways you have taught me to pray and thus enabled this book. Your life is a living prayer. I am grateful for you, and I am thankful that you are my mom. Equally to my dad, Rusty, thank you for finding ways to be faithful to the church that continue to inspire me. Your faithfulness is not in vain.

To Scott: God knew my life would be far less mundane when you came into the world. I'm grateful that you're not only my brother but also my friend. You've been there for me in the middle of the night from Paris to Statesville, and for that I'm forever in your debt.

To Dan and Mindy: Thank you for being the best friends a guy can have. Thank you for bearing with my midnight texts and late-night conversations. Though you may not see it, you have been Christ for me. To friends Frankie Boyko, The Rev. Sarah Heath, and Ruwa Romman, I am grateful that you are my people. You have shown me the heart of God.

To the Rev. Nathan Kirkpatrick: You have helped me think about God, Christ's church, and the Spirit's movement in my life in ways few others can. Thank you so very much.

To the communities and people who made this book possible: For Keith Gammons, the publisher who first believed in my work before I came to notoriety, I am so grateful. Leslie Andres and everyone at Smyth & Helwys Publishing, I am forever in your debt and am grateful to partner with you. To my team at the Holiday Inn-Charlotte Airport and especially the Hilton Garden Inn, Statesville, thank you for allowing a wayward pastor to work with you and learn from you. To Pacific School of Religion, thanks for allowing my writing to be incorporated into my doctoral work and for the ability to pursue both my doctorate and my writing career concurrently.

Finally, to my community of faith that our family attends, Broad Street United Methodist Church in Statesville: Thank you for continuing to be our church family. You keep showing up for me and reminding me of my place in the family of God.

CONTENTS

FOREWORD

So much of life happens at night.

We Christians who have inherited the great traditions of the Protestant Reformation have also internalized some unfortunate habits of thought. The Reformers thought of God as light, and they routinely pictured growing knowledge of God as illumination, being filled with light. In our hymns, sermons, and prayers night and darkness became synonymous with sin and death. Our tradition proposed that the life-giving time for work and purpose was the day.

In the wider and longer Christian tradition there have been other ways of figuring our encounter with God. For earlier theologians and mystics, God was perhaps most clearly to be found in the dark, in the mystery of human suffering and struggle. One of the constant modes of talking about God has been the *apophatic* way—describing God negatively by what we cannot say.

"All I know is a door into the dark." That is how poet Seamus Heaney begins "The Forge," a poem overtly about a blacksmith but more deeply about the process of self-discovery and making art. The sparks that fly off the anvil are visible to us only because they emerge from near total darkness. Like the theologians and mystics who preceded him, Heaney spent a lot of time in the dark and emerged with a compelling vision of life and its possibilities.

Luckily for us, Rob Lee has spent a lot of time there, too. Uniquely for a preacher and writer, Rob's "night job" has allowed him time to pursue his ministerial and scholarly vocations during the day. But he has been keenly observant during those hours, and the result is the gem-like prayers on offer in this prayerbook for night owls. He has seen life in all its nighttime manifestations, and his empathic imagination has allowed him to enter into the hearts and minds of those who, in the words of my church's prayerbook, "work or watch or weep" at night. The result is a collection of prayers that at once give voice to our own nighttime needs and open us up to what other people are going through as well. These prayers both speak for us and speak for others to us.

I recently had the opportunity to see a museum exhibit that put two contrasting Renaissance paintings in the same room. One pictured a saint receiving divine illumination from the sun. The other showed a philosopher looking intently into the dark. The spiritual life is like that. There is not only one way to encounter the divine. So the Reformers weren't wrong: God is light. But God is something else, too. Sometimes the light can overwhelm the things we are trying to see. The mystics weren't wrong, either:

God is unknowable, and is often revealed in what we cannot (or would not) take in.

Of all the thoughtful, prayerful people I know, Rob Lee is uniquely qualified to conceive and write a book like this. His life and ministry have led him into engagement with a range of people many of us in ministry only read and hear about. Rob is at once theologically learned, pastorally sensitive, and committed to an inclusive vision of God's liberating justice. The prayers here reflect his personal authenticity and active compassion. Using them in the spirit in which they are given will help each of us grow more fully into what Thomas Merton called our "authentic selves."

"All I know is a door into the dark." Rob Lee's prayers are little doorways into the dark of a night where both God and human need are revealed. They are keenly observed, compassionately expressed, and artfully written. This book is a gift from one who lives and works in that time of night of which most of us are unaware. God is up to something at night and up to something in this beautiful book. Receive it as the gift it is and use it as your own doorway into the ways in which God is working in the nights and days of your life. As we faithfully persevere in praying Rob's prayers you, I, and the world will be healed.

—*The Very Rev. Gary R. Hall, PhD*
President of Bloy House
The Episcopal School of Theology at Los Angeles
10th Dean of the Washington National Cathedral

INTRODUCTION

In August 2021, my wife and I had just adopted our two daughters, and I decided to leave my church job to care for them. The girls had family (both biological and foster) who were attending the church, and we needed space to become more fully a family unit without the trappings required by being a pastor in that environment. I knew deep down that I enjoyed working, and we needed my income in addition to my wife's income, so I took a job working the overnight shift at the local Hilton Garden Inn in my town. While at first it took adjustments and acclimations, it quickly became a job I enjoyed and found meaningful. I would work from 11 p.m. to 7 a.m. and then sleep for a bit while the girls were in school. When it was time to pick them up, I awoke and headed to their schools. This enabled me to continue my work of preaching across the country on issues that were important to me while also having a chance to try my hand at something new. There were times at first when the carefully laid plan failed miserably. I still live in the terror and shadow of the time I missed picking up my youngest daughter from her preschool. Thankfully, my parents live in our little town, and my dad had picked her up by the time I realized it.

We're further along now than we were when I started working third shift. I still really enjoy it, and I get to continue my preaching and teaching ministry as well. As time has passed, I notice that I pray during the quiet of the nighttime hours. As I do my hotel work, I plead with God to make time go faster so I can get home, or I beg God to make time slow down as I see my daughters growing with each passing day. I pray for Stephanie and all that she carries. I pray for the world, for the church, for those in harm's way. Every time a siren passes the hotel, I pray for the person who needs that assistance.

Here's the thing, though: I don't fancy myself a decent person of prayer. I try quite hard to be a good pray-er, but sometimes my prayer life looks more like a bomb site[1] than a serene piece of artwork. Yet Thomas Merton famously prayed, "I believe that the desire to please you does in fact please you."[2] Perhaps in these evening moments, God is employing the refiner's fire and the fuller's soap[3] to hone my prayer life in a way that I learn by trying. I learn to pray

---

1. I am indebted to the Rev. Dr. Sam Wells's imagery here, which he used in his sermon at the 86th Baccalaureate Service in 2012 at Duke University Divinity School.

2. Thomas Merton, *Thoughts in Solitude* (1956; repr. New York: Farrar, Straus and Giroux, 1999).

3. See Malachi 3:3: "he will sit as a refiner and purifier of silver, and he will purify the descendants of Levi and refine them like gold and silver, until they present offerings to the LORD in righteousness."

out of necessity—because in some quiet moments, prayer is all you have. I learn to pray because I need it. I hope you can hone your skills as well. Prayer is to be practiced, refined, and enacted. Just like the concept of sanctification, it is forever working itself out over the course of our lifetimes.

This book is both a practice journal and an exhibition of prayer that I have found to have meaning and cadence in my life. In a prayer life, I have discovered that rhythm is important. Over and over again, we return to God for a myriad of reasons. Those who find themselves up at night, for whatever reason, need prayer more than most. For the loneliness of the hour, the sadness of the moment, or simply the fact that most of the world is asleep while you go about your life, prayer is a succor and a balm in the wee hours. We would we be wise to practice and find vocabulary for prayer.

Does Prayer Work?

Many clergy get questions repeated in different forms and formats throughout their ministerial careers. The Rev. Dr. James C. Howell, a United Methodist pastor, once preached that he will never grow tired of holding someone's hand in the hospital as they lie dying, but he might one day be accused of jumping over the table and strangling someone who asks *yet again* if he is going to burn out due to holding someone's hand in the hospital.[4] For whatever reason, some questions are asked repeatedly. One of the questions I seem to be allotted is "Does prayer work?"—a valid question, but it presupposes that prayer has mechanisms or goals to accomplish.

While prayer takes different forms for different people, there are ways that prayer isn't as efficacious as it might be. It could be argued that the only way prayer *actually* works is when God's glory is made plain and visible. To suggest that prayer "works" because the outcome is ideal indicates that it may not be God answering prayer but the universe's uncanny ability to create circumstantial evidence.

Prayer works when God is glorified. The scary thing for us is that God's glory may look different than our desired outcome. It is also important to remember that God's on-time answer may be far different than our understanding of time and temporal realities. God always answers those who call on God. What a terribly beautiful and timely truth.

How You Might Use This Book

Prayerbooks are meant to be all-encompassing, yet they never are. This book should be held, digested, and edited as needed. Should a sentence that I've written seem off, you should adjust it for what you

---

4. This sermon was preached by the Rev. Dr. James C. Howell at the 2007 Western North Carolina Annual Conference of the United Methodist Church. The service was held on June 9, 2007.

need. Some prayerbooks are bound by church law to stay the same throughout time. This is not one of those books. Let it grow with you and be a guide that helps you through the night.

You may return to this book night after night for a certain prayer, or you may take it out to mark a certain occasion that is meaningful to you. You may use it as a devotional or as a communal resource. You may end up using it as a drink coaster on your bedside table until you realize you want to pray more. Regardless of how you use this book, it was written with you in mind. It was written in the spirit of both renewal and possibility, with not a word written in judgment or condescension. Nighttime worries do not have to define your existence, and no one should judge your prayer life. You should shape who you are by paying attention to the ways God calls you to follow in your Redeemer's footsteps. The night is a beautiful and promising time; it does not have to be full of anxiety. I hope this book will be a guidepost in the journey of realizing that though we are a first-shift world, there are people who live just as well in a third-shift reality. Third-shift lifestyles are just as rewarding, and those who work them are equally in need of prayer. We need forms of prayer and liturgies for experiencing God in the middle of the night as well. After all, the resurrection happened "early in the morning on the first day of the week while it was still dark" (John 20:1).

After the resurrection of Jesus, the church's fledgling years were forged in the darkness of catacombs, often under the cover of night when the authorities wouldn't be looking. Galileo challenged the work of the church because of what he saw at night. Harriet Tubman whispered hymns of freedom as she guided enslaved people north toward freedom. Soldiers' hushed prayers begging for protection were offered in the early morning hours as they prepared to liberate Europe in the final month of World War II. The first brick of the Stonewall riots that caused the nation to turn and reckon with its LGBTQ+ citizens was thrown in the nighttime hours. Things happen at night; we must only pay attention to see this is true.

What Does This Book Require?

If the clarion call for the community of faith is to pay attention, we must do so in the meaningful and the mundane moments. This book is meant for your individual reading and is worded as such because often things that happen in the night are done in lonely[5] fashion. Yet in our aloneness we find that God shows up in profoundly real ways. For so long, nighttime has been deemed less than, disgraced, or profane, but nighttime situations and scenarios demand the holy and beg for the Divine's presence. This book requires us to recognize that the night is as beautiful as the

---

5. In this instance, I do not mean lonely as in being without friends or loved ones—rather that the work of prayer at night is done alone.

day—they are just profoundly different and beautiful parts of the created order of God.

Finally, this book begs you to fear God. Not in the sense of God being vengeful or angry—I've long given up on that kind of god. You should fear that God might actually be sovereign enough to show up and be present for you in your moment of need. That causes me to tremble. It causes me to tremble because that kind of compassion is pure and holy. If we have the audacity to pray for God to show up at whatever hour, we had best be ready for what might come to pass when God does show up. This hope of God showing up has gotten many saints through their darkest nights. Don't be afraid to claim God but be mindful that God is about to show up to claim you. Are you ready for it?

PRAYERS FOR ALL
NIGHTTIME HOURS

A Blessing for a Bedroom

Bedrooms are sacred places of rejuvenation and revitalization. They are often private spaces, but they are incredibly important to us. This blessing, like all the prayers and liturgies in this book, should be adapted to suit the unique, individual situation and experience. Movement is important in any blessing, so suggested directions are offered in this short blessing.

> The LORD bless you and keep you;
> the LORD make his face to shine upon you and
> be gracious to you;
> the LORD lift up his countenance upon you and
> give you peace. (Numbers 6:24-26)

Blessing Notes: This blessing should be offered beginning at the doorpost of the room and then moving throughout the room. If more than one person is present, a person should be designated as liturgist or prayer leader, and the rest should follow in their footsteps.

Leader: Blessed are you, Lord God, who gives us rest and respite. In your love you made us, and in your love you guide our rest. Give blessing to this bedroom. May the bed be a place of comfort and restoration, may the lamps be gifts of light in the darkness, and may the walls stand strong against the weather.

Refrain: Keep watch, dear God.

Lord God, shield your servants who sleep in this space. Give them/us/me a sense of your goodness each night so that I might be equipped to share that goodness with those who come across the path of this life.

Refrain: Keep watch, dear God.

In the fullness of your grace, bring all things to completion, and at last give eternal rest. But until then, may this place be a shelter of the most high God. Endow this place with joy; insure this bedroom with your power. This we ask because you are watching and waiting this night for those who call on you.

ALL: Amen.

A Blessing for an Evening or Midnight Snack

We've all caught ourselves standing in front of a fridge and wondering what to concoct to get us through to breakfast. It may seem like a mundane act, but there is holiness in the mundane. God's glory is revealed in our midnight snacks, and we should give thanks for the gifts of sustenance bestowed upon us.

Jesus said to them, "I am the bread of life. Whoever comes to me will never be hungry, and whoever believes in me will never be thirsty." (John 6:35)

Gracious God,
You are the Lord of abundance and fruitfulness. In all things, you have given me so much. Bless this snack, small as it may be. May it be used for nourishment and strength so that I might praise you through my waking and my sleeping. Thank you, God. Amen.

A Child's Prayer for Night

Sometimes children see things in ways that we should see them, but we often don't. The prayers of the faithful rise to our God like sweet perfume regardless of their age, yet I am tempted to believe God's heart is especially concerned with the youngest voices praying prayers of supplication, thanksgiving, and conversation. The prayers I have heard my daughters pray have profound depth and thoughtfulness. God must delight in hearing such offerings.

Jesus said, "Let the children come to me, and do not stop them, for it is to such as these that the kingdom of heaven belongs." (Matthew 19:14)

Note: This prayer was written with the help of Phoenix (age five) and Athena (age six). They were happy to contribute to their dad's book.

Dear God,
It is night outside and the moon is out. Be with the people I love most. Help the world know that you love us so much. Be with my family and my pets; help them to have sweet dreams. If the night gets scary, help me. Thank you for loving me and not leaving me. I love you too—forever and always. Amen.

A Prayer at Dusk

As defined by the National Oceanic and Atmospheric Administration, dusk is the time when the sun no longer brightens the sky. It is the furthest point of twilight just before nightfall.[6] This liminal space between night and day is both beautiful and terrifying depending on your perspective. Liminal spaces are holy. We would be wise to pay attention in these moments, as God often shows up in the borderline spaces.

---

6. National Oceanic and Atmospheric Administration, forecast glossary, forecast.weather.gov/glossary.php?word=DUSK.

> It is the LORD who goes before you. He will be
> with you; he will not fail you or forsake you. Do
> not fear or be dismayed. (Deuteronomy 31:8)

God of the spaces in between,
In this moment of not-yet-night, keep me moored to
the promise that you will never leave me or forsake
me. May this night be both holy and good. May the
day behind me be held in context for what it was.
You are an ever-present help in trouble. If trouble
is ahead, be my guide and shield. But for now, let
me rest in the fullness of your grace. Thank you for
showing me your glory now and always. Amen.

A Prayer at Sunrise

As someone who works a job in the middle of the
night, I have found that sunrise is a blessing and a
challenge. Some days it feels liberating, as the ability
to rest is nigh. If it is a sleepless night for reasons
other than work, then sunrise spells challenge and
frustration as it requires us to rise to meet the day.
The mixture of providence and problem is part of
the human condition. Humanity has marveled at the
sunrise since before the dawn of time, and I imagine
some have dreaded it for just as long. It feels impos-
sible to face the moment of sunrise without prayer.
We dare not try.

> Blessed be the name of the LORD
>   from this time on and forevermore.
> From the rising of the sun to its setting,
>   the name of the LORD is to be praised.
> The LORD is high above all nations
>   and his glory above the heavens. (Psalm
>   113:2-4

There have been peoples from all times and religious persuasions who have worshiped the sun, Creator God. Yet I know that you are both Creator of the sun and Parent of the Son, our savior, Jesus Christ. As the sun comes up this morning, I ask your blessing on the day and all that it holds. As I pour my cup of coffee, do not neglect to pour your grace upon my steps this day. May compassion reign supreme, with joy the scepter and hope the footstool. May the sun rise for the sake of a new day, new possibility, and new wellsprings of grace. Amen.

A Prayer for an Evening Walk

Many of us take evening walks. What do you see? What do you hear? In typical fashion, as I get older, I find myself more interested in bird calls and other animal noises as I take my evening walk. In some ways, it's a symphony of sound and sensations. Part of the beauty of these sounds is that they all offer praise to the One who called them into being. I can think of no better posture to witness this concert than a posture of prayer.

> When he was at the table with them, he took bread, blessed and broke it, and gave it to them. Then their eyes were opened, and they recognized him, and he vanished from their sight. They said to each other, "Were not our hearts burning within us while he was talking to us on the road, while he was opening the scriptures to us?" That same hour they got up and returned to Jerusalem, and they found the eleven and their companions gathered together. They were saying, "The Lord has risen indeed, and he has appeared to Simon!" Then they told what had happened on the road and how he had been made known to them in the breaking of the bread. (Luke 24:30-35)

God of the world, I marvel at the brilliance and beauty of this twilight hour. As I walk through this community, remind me that you love this place too. You came to sanctify and save us all and redeem the whole of creation. As the night quickly approaches, bless this walk. May the journey be beautiful and the burden be light. This I ask as you journey with me all the days of my life. Thank you, dear God. Amen.

A Prayer for the Nearness of God

When I was a young child and felt sick, my mom would wrap me in a ladybug sleeping blanket that had belonged to her since her youth. In many ways it made me feel loved, cared for, and assured that things would be okay. To this day, my brother and I jokingly jab at each other over who will "inherit" the ladybug sleeping blanket. To me, it shows that proximity is important no matter the relationship. This is especially true for God. We were hardwired to want to be near to God, and we should always pray for that nearness.

> Let your gentleness be known to all. The Lord is near. (Philippians 4:5)

Dear Lord,

For so long I have cried to you—and this night feels no different. Come near, come close. My eyes are tired, and so is my soul. I've been going so hard, so fast, so long. Speak, Lord, and come near. Be for me the presence I need so that I might feel your touch closer than I feel my own self. Get up in my business, O God. Do not let me go. For you alone have brought this night to bear, and you alone will bring me through it. Give me rest and peace for tonight and for all the nights to come. Amen.

A Prayer for When You're in a Hotel Room

This book was conceived and birthed in a conference room of a hotel in Statesville, North Carolina. I worked as a night auditor for the hotel and found myself jotting down prayers that I wanted to save. Hotels are spaces that people share in fun and frivolity, but they are also incredibly lonely and sad. People often find themselves on their last leg, or on a business trip far from home. This prayer is for those who find themselves in a hotel, for whatever reason.

> And she brought forth her firstborn son, and wrapped him in swaddling clothes, and laid him in a manger; because there was no room for them in the inn. (Luke 2:7, King James Version)

God who longed for vacancy in Bethlehem,
This night I find myself in a place far from home, far from family, far from the creature comforts that I enjoy and crave. Give me peace and comfort tonight. Endow me with the ability to rest in a place that feels foreign and strange. You are a God who gives company to those who need it. I need you now. Bless the hotel workers and those here with me. Show them your compassion as well. I ask this in your name. Amen.

A Prayer for Writers Burning the Midnight Oil

Originally written for writers and those who commit pen to paper, or keystrokes to computer screen, this prayer is geared to those who wake up early or stay up late to write words that matter (even if only to them). But this prayer is possibly transcendent and appropriately adjustable for those who might need or want to do work in the middle of the night.

> And the one who was seated on the throne said, "See, I am making all things new." Also he said, "Write this, for these words are trustworthy and true." (Revelation 21:5)

God who is writing my story,
As I am writing away, may I be mindful that I am part of a priesthood of authors and professionals who have kept watch at this hour. I am not alone, and I stand on their shoulders. Though it is dark, Lord, let my vision be clear and concise—indeed, may my work be holy and whole. Keep those whom I love close at hand to your care. As I burn this midnight oil, may I be mindful of the oil in my lamp. May it burn for your glory, your honor, and your majesty, forever and ever. Thank you, Lord Christ, for the gift of this night and so many other gifts bestowed upon me. Amen.

A Prayer before Reading Scripture at Night

If you're like me, daytime can be chaotic for you. The only time I'm quiet enough to be in a posture to read Scripture is usually nighttime. This prayer of illumination seeks to celebrate both the glory of Scripture and the gift of a quiet moment. They seem so fleeting and few these days. Yet in these moments of reading Scripture, we are connected to the vast expanse of the Christian tradition and to our risen Lord. Let us not take that for granted.

> Thy word is a lamp unto my feet, and a light unto my path. (Psalm 119:105, King James Version)

Spirit of the Living God,
It seems silly to ask you to fall afresh on me at this hour when everything and everyone seems so tired. Yet in these quiet moments, I have a chance to read the Scripture you inspired as your own. I see you in the stories of Moses's call, of Elijah's despair, of Ruth's loyalty, and of Esther's bravery. I hear your call to David, to Nehemiah, and to Jeremiah. I see your persistence in Mary and Elizabeth and your righteous indignation in John the Baptizer. I see your pressing call in the works of Peter and Paul, and I see your vision-giving goodness in John of Patmos. Most of all, Lord, I see you in Jesus. I see you in the compassion poured out time and time again by your Son, our savior. Help these words to leap off the page so

that they might be fresh and new again this night and every night I open your abiding word. Thank you for this cherished gift. Amen.

A Prayer of Thanksgiving for a Good Day

It's easy to pray to God when things are going wrong. It's easy to forget to thank God and offer prayers of thanksgiving when things are going right. Yet in these moments of goodness, God desires to hear from us. Perhaps we could offer a prayer to show God our thanks, praise, and worship. In this spirit, we give this prayer of thanksgiving for a day that has been good.

> Rejoice always, pray without ceasing, give thanks in all circumstances, for this is the will of God in Christ Jesus for you. (1 Thessalonians 5:16-18)

O Lord, it is easy to become complacent in our complaining. But today was good. It was full. It was complete. Help me as your child to rest in the knowledge that you intend goodness for me, and I have every right to receive it. As this day is commended to history, help me look forward to other good days and other good things yet to come. Help me look forward to the good. Thank you, and Amen.

A Prayer When You See the Moon

Earth's Moon is the only place humans have set foot beyond our own planet. It is our natural satellite, helps control Earth's climate, and causes tides to go their way. It is the brightest and closest object in our night sky. For many, it is a companion and guide. We give thanks to God for the moon that lights the night sky and for God's goodness in setting it.

> Praise the LORD!
> Praise the LORD from the heavens;
>   praise him in the heights!
> Praise him, all his angels;
>   praise him, all his host!
> Praise him, sun and moon;
>   praise him, all you shining stars!
> Praise him, you highest heavens
>   and you waters above the heavens! (Psalm 148:1-4)

Great God of the night sky,
You gave us a moon to keep us company as the sun retreats. We give you thanks for its reflective powers and for how it has guided multitudes of saints and sinners along their way. Help us to find you in the moonlight.

You are both creative and inventive. You gave us a spirit of curiosity that caused us to lift from this plain to the heights of space. We made steps and forward movements to the places where none had yet gone. Keep us humble and keep us looking upward in wonder toward the beauty of what you gave us. This we ask because we are both curious and amazed. Amen.

Variations on "Now I Lay Me Down to Sleep"

The children's bedtime prayer is an essential part of many a child's bedtime routine. The earliest roots of the prayer are found in George Wheler's *The Protestant Monastery* written in 1698. The now-iconic version of the prayer was first found in *The New England Primer* and goes like this:

> Now I lay me down to sleep,
> I pray the Lord my soul to keep;
> If I should die before I wake,
> I pray the Lord my soul to take.

> If you sit down, you will not be afraid; when you lie down, your sleep will be sweet. (Proverbs 3:24)

Now I lay me down to sleep
God, this child is so precious, so sleepy, so fragile.

I pray the Lord my soul to keep

Keep them in your watch-care, God. This world is both broken and beautiful. Let them see the beauty amid the broken pieces of this turbulent existence.

If I should die before I wake

I know conceptually that you will care for them should the unthinkable happen, as you have cared for them their whole life long. But not yet, Lord God. Give them time in abundance.

I pray the Lord my soul to take

No matter the time we have left, grant that the proximity to you outweighs any pain we might experience. At our last breath, take us to that heavenly shore and keep us under the shelter of your wing in glory everlasting. We are bound for the kingdom, and we are grateful that you will bring us along. Amen.

PRAYERS FOR
DIFFICULT NIGHTS

If you're in crisis, please dial 988.

A Prayer for a Bad Dream

Bad dreams are often viewed as something only children experience. Yet we all know in the quiet of our hearts that nightmares can happen to adults, too. We are not immune to the power of dreams, and dreams that are frightful can cause us to awake with sweat dripping down our foreheads and fear streaking down our spines.

> You will not fear the terror of the night or the arrow that flies by day or the pestilence that stalks in darkness or the destruction that wastes at noonday. (Psalm 91:5-6)

Dear Jesus,
When you were on earth what did you dream about? Were they happy dreams? Did you dream of what the world might be if it only followed your path for it? Did you envision your kingdom that you left behind for our sake? Did you have nightmares? Did you see people hurting?

Lord, I had a dream this night, and it was not pleasant. Even though I am assured through the psalmist's words that I need not fear the terror of the night, it sure feels fearful. Help me to experience once more the assurance of your presence so I might find rest again. Please protect me from feeling that fear again and keep me from being entrapped in the power of dreams. This I ask in your strong name. Amen.

A Prayer for a Night Full of Financial Worry

Many of us longed to grow up, only to find that there are such things as sleepless nights surrounding financial woes and worries. Almost every family has times when it is difficult to make ends meet. We've all been there. Even so, it is an incredibly isolating and lonely space to be. God's assurance of being with us does not stop when the worries begin; in some ways, it intensifies.

> Look at the birds of the air: they neither sow nor reap nor gather into barns, and yet your heavenly Father feeds them. Are you not of more value than they? (Matthew 6:26)

Lord Christ, the love of money may be the root of all evil, but it is also the root of my worry too. This night, help me to see clearly what might be possible to solve this problem I face. As I lie here, may the problems that persist fade in the presence of your glory. Help me find your will amid the fray of this turbulent life. This too shall pass. I shall yet prevail by your grace. For that I am thankful. Amen.

A Prayer for a Stormy Night

Not too long ago, my town was in the path of a terrible storm. Our family gathered in a closet as the storm ripped through our community. It was terrifying for everyone, and there were frightful moments when I found myself praying more fervently than I had in a long time. Large trees fell, but our home was spared large-scale damage. Even still, my youngest daughter remains fearful when thunder rolls through. This prayer is for those nights when storms are raging.

> One day he got into a boat with his disciples, and he said to them, "Let us go across to the other side of the lake." So they put out, and while they were sailing he fell asleep. A windstorm swept down on the lake, and the boat was filling with water, and they were in danger. They went to him and woke him up, shouting, "Master, Master, we are perishing!" And waking up, he rebuked the wind and the raging waves; they ceased, and there was a calm. Then he said to them, "Where is your faith?" They were terrified and amazed and said to one another, "Who then is this, that he commands even the winds and the water and they obey him?" (Luke 8:22-25)

Lord Jesus, what was it like to calm the storm?

Were you dreaming when the storm raged that day on the water? Was it dark as night when the storm began to pound? Right now, it feels like I can't catch a break. Here I am in the middle of the night, and there seems to be little to turn to and no one to cling to as the thunder claps and lightning fills the night sky. It is in this moment that I hold fast to you, O Solid Rock. All other ground is sinking sand, all other ground is sinking sand. Keep us safe. Amen.

A Prayer for Anxious Nights

When I was in middle school at a private Christian school, I vividly remember a fellow student telling me that being anxious was a sin based on St. Paul's words to the church at Philippi in Philippians 4. This notion of anxiety as sin scared me. It scared me because anxiety dwelt intimately within me and knew me well. To suggest this aspect of me was innately sinful only gave me more anxiety, thus more sin. Was this what my life was to become? Sin upon sin because my mind couldn't slow down quickly enough?

This is the power of anxiety over people, including myself. God's intent for us is not to worry that our worry might be sin but rather to trust in the goodness of God. God's goodness overpowers our anxiety, and we find ourselves safe in the cleft meant for each of us. Anxiety isn't sin, but it is met with the full force of God's love, grace, and abundance in the nighttime hours and all day long.

Do not be anxious about anything, but in everything by prayer and supplication with thanksgiving let your requests be made known to God. And the peace of God, which surpasses all understanding, will guard your hearts and your minds in Christ Jesus. (Philippians 4:6-7)

We long to be calm, O God.
Soothe our spirits with your Spirit.
We long to be at peace, Lord Christ.
Soothe our spirits with your Spirit.
In your goodness, do not let me shiver with fear or wrestle with my anxieties forever.
Soothe our spirits with your Spirit.
In your charity, remind me that I am not alone. I am surrounded by a detachment of grace from the very throne of God.
Soothe our spirits with your Spirit.
This isn't easy. This is a difficult road laid before me. Must I go alone?
No! In all these things I am more than a conqueror through my Lord who loves me. Thanks be to God. AMEN!

A Prayer for Incomplete Work

For me and maybe for you, most nights feel incomplete as we long for something we don't have. There is so much to do during the day that often it spills into our nighttime routines. We want to complete our checklists, yet we know we can only do that if we rest. The longing for rest, for real rest, for sabbath rest is part of realizing that incomplete work has its place, but it does not define who we are or what we long to be. As children of God, may we feel that even in with our incomplete work we are made complete through Christ.

> As the Father has loved me, so I have loved you; abide in my love. If you keep my commandments, you will abide in my love, just as I have kept my Father's commandments and abide in his love. I have said these things to you so that my joy may be in you and that your joy may be complete. (John 15:9-11)

Completing and Finishing God,
You brought forth something out of nothing as you swept across the dark waters. You caused order out of chaos and gave purpose to that which had none. Yet even still I work for deadlines and projects to get to where I want to be. I work hard and forget so often that you are a God who will complete things. In my longing to be complete, I sometimes forget that you have completed the work of sanctification for us. And that act is more than just a check off my checklist. You are working to sanctify me for the work of your kingdom. May all this be completed for the day of your coming. This we ask in the name of the one who said, "It is finished"—Jesus Christ, our Lord. Amen.

A Prayer for Lonely Nights

Many of us have had a lonely night that never seemed to end. We found ourselves on a work trip, or at the end of a long relationship, or after dropping a child off for college. Such moments can feel incredibly isolating, intimidating, and disorienting. We need God in those lonely moments. The comforting truth is that God knows what lonely nights look like. On the night before Jesus gave himself up for us, he spent agonizing hours of lonely prayer in a garden as the ones he knew as friends slept idly by. The old hymn even says, "Jesus walked that lonesome valley."[7] Just as we walk our own lonesome roads, we trust that Christ too walked a road in the ultimate act of solidarity to show God's love for us.

> Then Jesus went with them to a place called Gethsemane, and he said to his disciples, "Sit here while I go over there and pray." He took with him Peter and the two sons of Zebedee and began to be grieved and agitated. Then he said to them, "My soul is deeply grieved, even to death; remain here, and stay awake with me." And going a little farther, he threw himself on the ground and prayed, "My Father, if it is possible, let this

---

7. "Jesus Walked This Lonesome Valley," American folk hymn, author unknown.

cup pass from me, yet not what I want but what you want." Then he came to the disciples and found them sleeping, and he said to Peter, "So, could you not stay awake with me one hour? Stay awake and pray that you may not come into the time of trial; the spirit indeed is willing, but the flesh is weak." Again he went away for the second time and prayed, "My Father, if this cannot pass unless I drink it, your will be done." Again he came and found them sleeping, for their eyes were heavy. So, leaving them again, he went away and prayed for the third time, saying the same words. Then he came to the disciples and said to them, "Are you still sleeping and taking your rest? Now the hour is at hand, and the Son of Man is betrayed into the hands of sinners. Get up, let us be going. Look, my betrayer is at hand." (Matthew 26:36-46)

Abiding Christ, savior and friend,
You knew loneliness and knew it well. Keep me close this night. The darkness feels isolating. The night feels suffocating. In your charity, be with those whom I love. They may not be here right now, but they are in your watch-care. Give them grace sufficient for this hour, and since your grace is without limit or scope, give me a portion too. You might want to make it a double portion based on how I feel right now. But my trust remains in you, Lord God. As nighttime turns to day, I will continue to sing of your works because you brought me out of the pit to a place of honor. You are a God who hears. Hear me now. Amen.

A Prayer for Restless Nights

St. Augustine said that our hearts are restless until they find rest in God. Our tendency is to force rest rather than seek the calm and tranquility we desire. Perhaps this prayer will help you find God and rest in tandem. Perhaps one will lead to the other. Either way, God will show up in God's own timing and way. God does not forget God's children—especially those who feel restless tonight.

> But the Advocate, the Holy Spirit, whom the Father will send in my name, will teach you everything and remind you of all that I have said to you. Peace I leave with you; my peace I give to you. I do not give to you as the world gives. Do not let your hearts be troubled, and do not let them be afraid. (John 14:26-27)

God, who brought forth night and darkness from the primordial waters, sometimes it feels like night is easier to come by than day. When it comes time to close my eyes, I can't seem to do it. It's frustrating, it's disorienting, it's disheartening. Sit with me in my weariness, O Lord. Do not forsake me. Allow me to rest. Let my heart rest in you. Let my body rest in this space. Let the holiness of night not be lost on me. In the name of the one who rested in the storm. Amen.

A Prayer for the Nights in the Gutter (based on Oscar Wilde's line)

Oscar Wilde famously wrote, "We are all in the gutter, but some of us are looking at the stars."[8] That line has always resonated with me. It is the assurance that our location does not determine our vision or predict where our location might be later in the narrative. God is not done yet. We should keep our eyes heavenward.

> The one who made the Pleiades and Orion and turns deep darkness into the morning and darkens the day into night, who calls for the water of the sea and pours it out on the surface of the earth, the LORD is his name. (Amos 5:8)

Lord of the gutter,
Train my vision toward the stars lest I lose sight of your intent for my life, my livelihood, and my calling. The gutter is not my station, yet it is where I am, so may it be a place of blessing even if it doesn't appear that way. May I rise from the place I am to the place you intend for me to be. Raise me now and raise

---

8. Oscar Wilde, *Lady Windermere's Fan*, 1893.

me on the Last Day, so that in all things I might be drawn to where you are. Thanks be to God. Amen.

A Prayer for When You Didn't Get Enough Sleep

In the 2023 blockbuster film *Barbie*, there's a scene where Barbie (played by Margot Robbie) clearly didn't get enough sleep. For Barbie, her feeling of exhaustion is a sure sign that something is incredibly wrong in her world. It requires her to both address and face realities that she never intended to address— including the possibility that she is malfunctioning. It may seem like hyperbole, but missing out on a good night's rest is both problematic and a sign of malfunctioning on our part. And it happens to all of us. Sometimes we struggle to rest. This prayer is for those nights.

> Where can I go from your spirit? Or where can I flee from your presence? If I ascend to heaven, you are there; if I make my bed in Sheol, you are there. If I take the wings of the morning and settle at the farthest limits of the sea, even there your hand shall lead me, and your right hand shall hold me fast. (Psalm 139:7-10)

Jesus my Lord,

You know what it is like to be fully human even as you always remain fully divine. That last night before you gave yourself up for us, you stayed up and kept watch while others slept soundly. You know what I'm going through. Stay near to me now. It's frustrating and confusing. It's infuriating and disheartening.

As the sleepless night turns to morning light, may my patience be full, may my hope be renewed, and may my empathy be fruitful. Thank you for showing me the way to get through this. I couldn't do it without you. Amen.

A Prayer of Supplication for a Bad Day

We can't always prevent bad days. Things go wrong, and try as we might, we can't always leave the bad things behind when night falls. Bad days sometimes turn into bad weeks, months, and seasons of our lives. God pleads with us to allow God's presence to go before us and accompany us along life's way—bad days and all. Sometimes it's difficult to hear the still, small voice of God in in daily life, yet there in the middle of it all stands a Savior ready to lend aid.

> My little children, I am writing these things to you so that you may not sin. But if anyone does

sin, we have an advocate with the Father, Jesus Christ the righteous, and he is the atoning sacrifice for our sins, and not for ours only but also for the sins of the whole world. (1 John 2:1-2)

Saving God, your kindness towards us is as abundant as your grace. Thank you that even in our failings you assure us of the good, the beautiful, and the sublime. In this series of bad days that I'm experiencing, help me to hear your voice clearly and directly. Revive this moment for the sake of your servant and for the mission you have in the world. In your mercy, give me respite from the storm outside and shelter amid the wind and rain. When at last the bad days pass and the sun returns in the morning, do not let me forget what you have done for me. You have not abandoned your child, and that means the world. Amen and amen.

A Prayer for When You Didn't Sleep

For many, the feeling of a lack of sleep is demoralizing and disappointing on multiple levels. Try as we might to have rested, we find ourselves hitting the snooze button over and over and over. Or perhaps you are at work or school, longing for the bed that you were forced to leave because duty called.

Whatever the case, sleep is important, necessary, and good. According to the Center for Disease Control and Prevention, one in three adults in the United States reports not getting enough sleep every night.[9] If this is such a common problem, there should be a prayer to offer for long days with no rest in sight.

> The LORD is my shepherd; I shall not want.
> He maketh me to lie down in green pastures: he leadeth me beside the still waters.
> He restoreth my soul: he leadeth me in the paths of righteousness for his name's sake. (Psalm 23:1-3, KJV)

God, take this day and do something with it.
Take it and make it something because at this point I just can't.
Don't forget that I have that meeting, that test, that encounter that can't go wrong.
I feel like it's going to go wrong. I just can't do this anymore, because doing it would require me to be fully present, and I am not.
    And yet . . .
    I am here and will make a way because I trust in you. You made a way out of no way. You brought dead folks back to life. Lord, in my feelings that are akin to a mini death, might you do for me what you did for them? Raise me to new vigor and strength, as you will do for me on the last day. I can do this . . . no, God, *we* can do this. Let's get it done. Amen.

---

9. National Institutes of Health, "What Are Sleep Deprivation and Deficiency?" www.nhlbi.nih.gov/health/sleep-deprivation.

An Insomniac's Prayer

According to the National Institute of Health, insomnia is a common sleep disorder in which someone has trouble falling asleep, staying asleep, or getting good quality sleep, despite the environmental conditions being conducive for sleep. Chronic insomnia occurs three nights a week, lasts more than three months, and is not explained by any other extenuating circumstances.[10]

> Come to me, all you who are weary and are carrying heavy burdens, and I will give you rest. (Matthew 11:28)

God who doesn't rest,

Even in your might you identify with me. You know me well, don't you? I wish that I was as powerful sometimes, with the ability to command rest and sleep. I would do that right now. Right now, I'm not going to ask for sleep, though I desire it. I ask that my lack of sleep might prove praise to your glory and might. Your glory is both magnificent and telling. Give me grace to experience rest when it does come and forgiveness for myself when the restful hours

---

10. National Institutes of Health, "What Is Insomnia?" www. nhlbi.nih.gov/health/insomnia.

don't add up the way I think they ought to. Show me your glory, God of all things; pass by me now. Amen.

PRAYERS FOR OTHERS

A Prayer for a Friend on Your Mind This Night

Friendship is everything to me. I work hard to be a good friend. There are times when I have failed miserably at my endeavors in friendship and times when I have risen to what the occasion demanded. Through it all, I've believed that God shows up in friendships through the ways we love one another. Friendship deserves more credit than it often receives in our hyper-romanticized world. It is incumbent on us to pray for friends who are close to our hearts. I find it useful to pray for a friend whenever they come to mind, no matter the hour. You might pray this prayer for your friend during the night.

> A friend loves at all times, and kinsfolk are born to share adversity. (Proverbs 17:17)

Holy God,
Your son called his disciples friends. Throughout the Old and New Testaments are examples of true and generous friendship. In the Trinity, you find friendship in the Godhead. Be with my friend [friend's name] this night. They may not know I am thinking of them, but allow them to be assured of my well wishes and goodwill. Give them peace, extend to them the compassion you feel for them, and remind them that they have my love too. As we face each new tomorrow, may we do so together. Help them, Lord, and help me too. Your friendship toward your people

is an example we abide by. In your name, our friend, we pray. Amen.

A Prayer for a Pet as They Sleep

Many of us may not recognize how much pets see of us in our day-to-day lives. Our furry friends see us at our best and indeed are often right beside us at our worst. While some Christians don't believe in the redemption of animals and their ultimate salvation, the famed evangelist and priest John Wesley thought otherwise (as have countless other saints across the ages). In his sermon titled "The General Deliverance,"[11] Wesley proclaimed that if all creation is groaning for the newness offered in Christ as Romans says, then God will bring about redemption for the "brute" animal. God will restore even them. After all, they didn't get us into this mess. We should pray for them too.

> For the creation waits with eager longing for the revealing of the children of God, for the creation was subjected to futility, not of its own will, but by the will of the one who subjected it, in hope that the creation itself will be set free from its enslavement to decay and will obtain the freedom of the glory of the children of God. We know that

11. John Wesley, "The General Deliverance," 1781.

the whole creation has been groaning together as it suffers together the pains of labor, and not only the creation, but we ourselves, who have the first fruits of the Spirit, groan inwardly while we wait for adoption, the redemption of our bodies. (Romans 8:19-23)

Lord Christ, you gave us friends of all varieties. This night as I look lovingly at my pet, I give thanks that they feel safe here in this place. It's a cold world out there, and I'm grateful I get to help them feel the warmth of love and companionship for their time on this earth. I acknowledge there are animals without a home or a person to love and care for them. Give them the peace of your comfort, God of all creation. As we wait with eager longing for the restoration of all good things, may we cling to those good pets we have. Let them remind us of your plans for salvation for the world. Give [pet's name] and all animals rest this night, and give them joy in the morning. Amen.

A Prayer for a Teenager Sleeping in the Next Room

Looking over the trajectory and course of my life over the past thirty-plus years, I can confidently say that being a teenager is one of the most daunting realities any person has to face—at least in the moment of facing such reality. As I reflect now, I have had plenty of challenges far more discouraging or disillusioning, yet in the moment, being a teenager is quite difficult. Society requires you to be adult-like even though you are not afforded the privileges of being one. You go through hormonal changes and are interjected into social situations that are either foreign or make little sense. All this makes sleeping while your teenage child sleeps in the next room a tall order, one that needs prayer and assurance from God.

> Train children in the right way, and when old, they will not stray. (Proverbs 22:6)

Almighty God,

You watch over your children so that we might be secure in this life. Please watch over my teenager in the next room. They have grown so much, and you know they have so much growing left to do. Give them peace and serenity as they transition from childhood into the life you intend for them. There are many pressures and realities they face that I may not fully understand, so give me patience and courage to begin to learn. In the interim, keep us all at rest in the knowledge of your great love for us. I give you glory and thanks. Amen.

A Prayer for My Parents As They Sleep

Parenting is hard. Being in relationship with one's parents is a difficult reality for many within communities across the world. Power dynamics, misunderstandings, and mishandling of situations prove that parents are profoundly human in need of a Savior. For some children, it can be difficult to find inspired prayers for their parents. For others, parents have shown up for them in many ways. It is a mixed bag. Yet God is a big God and can bear these things in tension. May the prayers offered be lifted up to God for the sake of thanksgiving and healing.

> Children, obey your parents in the Lord, for this is right. "Honor your father and mother"—this is the first commandment with a promise—"so that it may be well with you and you may live long on the earth." And parents,[12] do not provoke your children to anger, but bring them up in the discipline and instruction of the Lord. (Ephesians 6:1-4)

God who is Father and Mother of us all,
You gave us the gift of parents. Give me a spirit of thanksgiving for the gifts they have offered me throughout the course of my life thus far. As they sleep this night, may they be surrounded by the feeling of love and abundant grace. If they are fearing

---

12. Edited from the original English word "fathers."

anything, calm them as they once sought to soothe me. If they are ailing in health or mind, give them peace that they give me when I am in their presence. Love on them, Lord God. If there is any animosity between them and someone else (even me), remove it and renew them. I thank you for them. Amen.

A Prayer for My Partner As They Sleep

We go through life with many relationship dynamics, some of them more intimate than others. The most intimate is the one we have with our partner, the person we choose to share life with. In this partnership, we may find ourselves close to one another during sleep and the nighttime hours. Sometimes they snore, other times they talk in their sleep, sometimes they are awake while we sleep, or we are up as they slumber. In these moments of vulnerability, we see how God is amid it all. God is weaving together the tapestry of our lives in a way that we are blessed by the presence of the person we love most.

> Set me as a seal upon your heart, as a seal upon your arm, for love is strong as death, passion fierce as the grave. Its flashes are flashes of fire, a raging flame. Many waters cannot quench love, neither can floods drown it. If one offered for

love all the wealth of one's house, it would be utterly scorned. (Song of Songs 8:6-7)

God whose love reigns and sustains,
You gave me my spouse/partner in your infinite compassion for me. You show me the power of love when I look at them and the beauty of grace when I think of them. The hope they engender in me is reflective of your glory, and so I give thanks. In your charity, grant them safe lodging tonight in their sleep. Remind them of yours and my love for them in their dreaming, so that in everything you may be glorified through your Son Jesus Christ, who with you and the Holy Spirit lives and reigns as one God, forever and ever. Amen.

A Prayer for Those Traveling at Night

We've all been there: traveling in the middle of the night, longing for home. As our eyes become blurry with tiredness, we wish for the sleep we've been missing for too long. And in humankind there is a line between people—you either don't mind traveling in the middle of the night, or you despise traveling at night. Whatever the case, we must be attuned to the ways the Spirit might speak to us in the midst of our travel.

PS—Be safe, too.

> Finally, brothers and sisters, whatever is true, whatever is honorable, whatever is just, whatever is pure, whatever is pleasing, whatever is commendable, if there is any excellence and if there is anything worthy of praise, think about these things. (Philippians 4:8)

Dear God,

I know you travel highways, byways, roadways, and alleyways to reach us. You will stop at nothing to bring us together with your goodness. You know that this night I am to travel the roadways/airways/railways/seaways of this great world you created. Keep me safe and keep me secure. Most importantly, keep me alert, both to my surroundings and to the ways you might show up for my well-being. As I travel, keep close to your heart those whom I love who are not with me. I hope they are resting and sleeping well. Thank you for your steadfastness and presence that does not fail. Thank you that your love is geo-located to my heart. May it be a beacon for others too. Amen.

A Prayer for Those Who Work at Night

We live in a first-shift world, and this is often proven to me when I receive phone calls during my precious sleeping hours in the morning. Yet despite the proclivity toward 9am to 5pm jobs, some of us make sure the world keeps turning while others sleep. It is daunting work, and it can be quite lonely no matter the trade. In my own work, I've learned to lean into West Coast friendships, but even that only goes so far. Perhaps we should keep these amazing souls who labor at night more on our minds than we do. We should certainly hold them in prayer.

> Therefore, keep awake, for you do not know when the master of the house will come, in the evening or at midnight or at cockcrow or at dawn, or else he may find you asleep when he comes suddenly. And what I say to you I say to all: Keep awake. (Mark 13:35-37)

Great Spirit,
You called nighttime into being before time began, and you called it good. You were a night owl when you graced this planet, our home. You will raise us at last to a place where there is no more nighttime, but until then there are those who labor on your behalf at night. Bless those who work this night so that they might know your goodness and presence. Keep those who labor safe, and defend them from the dangers of

their work and of the night. We give thanks for the ways these folks help our world, and we offer earnest intentions on their behalf. Amen.

A Prayer for Young Children Sleeping in the Next Room

When I was in the process of adopting my two daughters, I was told that it would be the first time my heart would live outside my body. I didn't believe this until I held my children in my arms the first night they were in my home. It was that sudden and that complete. While I acknowledge that families take different forms and shapes for different people, if your family includes children, you find yourself praying for them at all hours and in a myriad of ways.

> Jesus said, "Let the children come to me, and do not stop them, for it is to such as these that the kingdom of heaven belongs." (Matthew 19:14)

Eternal God,
Your son, our savior Jesus, once said that the little children should come to him, and we shouldn't hinder them. Right now, I worry for my children as I sit here awake and anxious for their future. Each child has so much ahead of them, and yet I feel that the future of the world is uncertain. It all seems too much. As you

guide their path, remind them of my love for them that is born of your great love for them. Let them grow in the knowledge of your love, grace, and steadfastness. The world needs you, God. That child needs you, God. Please don't let us down. Amen.

PRAYERS FOR
PEACE & SAFETY

A Prayer for a Night in the Hospital

Hospitals are important places in our society, as they help us experience healing and wholeness. But anyone who has spent a night in the hospital knows that they are places where comfortable sleeping conditions are hard to find and rest seems fleeting. In that crucible of discomfort and fear, we need God the most. In the fear, in the sickness, in the silence, and in the pain, we seek God's face.

> Are any among you sick? They should call for the elders of the church and have them pray over them, anointing them with oil in the name of the Lord. (James 5:14)

Spirit of Truth and Compassion,
You have often been called the Great Physician in moments like this. In some ways, you feel closer to me than the machines that surround us in this room. Great God of healing and wholeness, make known to me your presence, and lend me your aid in this moment. Do not let your nearness depart from my heart. I desire healing, Lord Christ, but give me wholeness above all else so that in everything my feet may be firmly planted in your salvation. Amen.

A Prayer for First Responders and Those in Harm's Way

My brother-in-law is a police officer, my cousin is a state trooper, and another cousin is a firefighter. They, along with many others, work hard to keep our communities safe. Though there are times when people in these professions have fallen painfully short, we still rely on their ability to show up for us at some of our most traumatic and painful moments. We should hold them in prayer and keep them close to our hearts.

> Do not fear, for I am with you; do not be afraid, for I am your God; I will strengthen you; I will help you; I will uphold you with my victorious right hand. (Isaiah 41:10)

God who preserves and defends,
Please protect those who are in harm's way this night. Keep those who serve our community under your careful eye. Provide a hedge of protection around them, and be especially with those who love them. Keep them accountable to their work, and do not allow the forces of wickedness to overtake them. The principalities and powers of this world may be great, but you are far greater. Do not forsake your servants. Do not forget them in their hour of work and toil. Bring them home safe, please. This we ask in the strong name of our Lord. Amen.

A Prayer for Those Experiencing Homelessness at Night

According to the National Alliance to End Homelessness, more than 500,000 people experienced homelessness during calendar year 2022, with 22 percent of that number chronically homeless (having experienced homelessness or homeless factors multiple times in their lives), 6 percent United States military veterans, and 5 percent considered vulnerable youth (under the age of twenty-five).[13]

In our fast-paced world, it is easy to forget those who experience homelessness in our communities or to let them fade into the background. The even more pernicious reality is the indictment and condemnation of those without houses in our hamlets, towns, and cities. However, God makes it clear that those who are suffering are close to God's heart and mind. If they are close to the heart of God, then they should be close to our hearts as well.

Religion that is pure and undefiled before God the Father is this: to care for orphans and widows

---

13. National Alliance to End Homelessness, "State of Homelessness: 2023 Edition," endhomelessness.org/homelessness-in-america/homelessness-statistics/state-of-homelessness/.

in their distress and to keep oneself unstained by
the world. (James 1:27)

God who set the stars on their courses,
You wandered in the first century as someone
"without a place to lay his head" (Matthew 8:20).
You know what those who are without homes this
night are feeling. Help me to have empathy for their
plight and respect for their human dignity. Hear their
prayers and cries for help, and bestow upon them the
fullness of your presence. Help us all to realize our
common humanity—and equally help us to demand
reforms that lead to lasting change for those experiencing homelessness in my community. This I pray
in the name of the one who is our home and our
rock, Jesus Christ, our Lord. Amen.

A Prayer for Those in Hospice Care

Hospice and palliative care often get a bad rap in this
country. This is because people assume that death is
imminent and pressing when that is not always the
case. Often, this kind of care simply signals that a life
is heading toward completion and an end. It requires
difficult decisions, heartfelt conversations, and senti-
mental goodbyes. Though the moments are fraught
with sadness, they have the potential to be holy. This

prayer invokes God's presence for those in hospice care and those who care for them.

> For everything there is a season and a time for
> every matter under heaven:
> a time to be born and a time to die;
> a time to plant and a time to pluck up what is
> planted;
> a time to kill and a time to heal;
> a time to break down and a time to build up;
> a time to weep and a time to laugh;
> a time to mourn and a time to dance;
> a time to throw away stones and a time to gather
> stones together;
> a time to embrace and a time to refrain from
> embracing;
> a time to seek and a time to lose;
> a time to keep and a time to throw away;
> a time to tear and a time to sew;
> a time to keep silent and a time to speak;
> a time to love and a time to hate;
> a time for war and a time for peace. (Ecclesiastes
> 3:1-8)

In the fullness of our time, great God, you will bring all of us to yourself. In this moment, I grieve for those surrounding [person's name] on their journey home. Keep them calm and filled with the knowledge of your amazing love. As they see your face come into focus, allow them the certainty of your promise to them never to leave their side. As the shadows become darkness like the night we are in now, remind them of the relationships that were precious to them here.

Enable those relationships to be precious in the here-after as well.

Lord, I dare not speculate on the specifics of where they are going—what it looks like and the karat of the streets of gold. Even still, may you also assure me that you've got this. I feel painfully out of control in [person's name] final hours. As we all struggle with what is to come, help us focus on what matters most: the grace you gave us through Jesus Christ, our judge and our hope. Amen.

A Prayer for Those in Prison Overnight

It's always astounding to me that Jesus makes it clear that we should visit and pray for those in prison, yet we are good at ignoring that command. If you've ever known someone who ended up in prison, you know it can be disorienting and heartbreaking. God's presence is never-wavering, though, no matter how heinous the alleged crime.

> [Jesus said,] "Then the king will say to those at his right hand, 'Come, you who are blessed by my Father, inherit the kingdom prepared for you from the foundation of the world, for I was hungry and you gave me food, I was thirsty and you gave me something to drink, I was a stranger

and you welcomed me, I was naked and you gave me clothing, I was sick and you took care of me, I was in prison and you visited me.' Then the righteous will answer him, 'Lord, when was it that we saw you hungry and gave you food or thirsty and gave you something to drink? And when was it that we saw you a stranger and welcomed you or naked and gave you clothing? And when was it that we saw you sick or in prison and visited you?' And the king will answer them, 'Truly I tell you, just as you did it to one of the least of these brothers and sisters of mine, you did it to me.'"
(Matthew 25:34-40)

God whose love knows no bounds,
This night I pray for [person's name] and all those in prison who are scared, confused, and lonely. Help them to feel the sanctifying and life-altering force of your great love. I know you won't give up on them, God, so help me not to give up on them either. Be with those who watch over them and have oversight to care for them. I call on you for help, O Lord. Help them in their time of need. Amen.

A Prayer for Those in a Psychiatric Facility, Hospital, or Ward

In many seminaries, students are taught what never to say when rendering pastoral care: "I know what you're going through." This statement makes it seems like you are making assumptions about the person's situation or circumstances. However, in this instance, I can say with full assurance of personal experience that I know what it's like to be in a psychiatric ward. For someone diagnosed with bipolar disorder, places like that come with the territory. In desperate moments, people who are hospitalized need your prayers. Grant them that gift to earnestly pray for them, their health, and those who care for them.

> O Lord, by these things people live, and in all these is the life of my spirit. Oh, restore me to health and make me live! Surely it was for my welfare that I had great bitterness, but you have held back my life from the pit of destruction, for you have cast all my sins behind your back. (Isaiah 38:16-17)

Lord God, by your incarnation you felt the full experience of being human. I sometimes wonder if that meant you knew what it felt like to lose your mind. I know you know what is going on, but it feels so strange to name it out loud. Be with your servant in psychiatric care this night. Assure them over and over and over again that you are with them and will never leave them or forsake them. Surround their caregivers and those they love most because none of this is easy or logical. Bring order out of this chaos in both their mind and their scenario. You alone can inspire the solution we so desperately need. Help. Amen.

A Prayer for Those Mourning during the Night

Night seems to lend itself to mourning. The pain of days past seems fresh and renewed as we are at our seemingly weakest moments. We can't help bringing to mind the sadness, the desolation of our existence, and the painstaking realization that this depth of despair is not leaving anytime soon. But God does not abandon us in our despair. Take heart: God is calling you to understand better how God will show up for you in this moment and bring peace in your storm.

> Weeping may linger for the night, but joy comes with the morning. (Psalm 30:5b)

Lord Christ, you wept in the garden and felt painfully alone. Yet in the bonds of the Trinity, you were never alone. We too feel the despair of aloneness in our weeping and in our mourning. Strengthen our bonds to you so we might feel the assurance of grace that is everlasting and complete. Complete in us our grief so we might feel once more the sunrise of joy that is on the horizon. We await the coming light. Amen.

A Prayer for Those Who Die during the Night

The nineteenth-century poet Emily Dickinson famously penned, "Because I could not stop for Death — / He kindly stopped for me."[14] The words ring true day or night; we are all bound for the grave. Yet our hope as Christians is not found as we go down to the grave but rather in the certainty that God has made right what once was wrong. Our resurrection hope is abiding, but that does not negate our grief as we remain on earth while those we love die into God. This prayer is for those who die during the night. It may be offered either at the exact time of death or upon discovery of the death. It should be noted that death is not easy or kind, but God's yoke and burden are easy and light. We die into the goodness of God.

---

14. Emily Dickinson, "Because I Could Not Stop for Death—479," *The Poems of Emily Dickinson*, ed. Ralph W. Franklin (Cambridge MA: Belknap Press of Harvard University Press).

"Do not let your hearts be troubled. Believe in God; believe also in me. In my Father's house there are many mansions. If it were not so, would I have told you that I go to prepare a place for you? And if I go and prepare a place for you, I will come again and will take you to myself, so that where I am, there you may be also. And you know the way to the place where I am going." (John 14:1-4, edited)[15]

Eternal Father, strong to save,[16]
You have led your servant to the place where you are. I give thanks that they are now safe in your embrace forever. Yet this moment feels so earth-shattering, so final. Send your assurance of life abundant meant for us all. Thank you for the ways that [person's name] showed me your presence and reflected your compassion. I give them back to your love and care now. Sanctify them and make them part of your perfect kingdom. Sanctify me also for the work of grief, remembrance, and reflection. Finally, on the Last Day raise our bodies, theirs and mine, to glory everlasting. Thank you for a life well lived. Thank you for the chance to experience their life. It is all grace. Amen.

---

15. In this portion of text, I reverted words from John 14:2 back to the King James Version. Instead of "dwelling places" as found in the NRSV (updated), it instead reads "mansions." The rest of the text is unaltered.

16. Adapted from William Whiting's "Eternal Father, Strong to Save" hymn lyrics. This hymn is also known as the Navy Hymn.

A Prayer for When News Breaks in the Middle of the Night

I wonder if you're like me and often fumble and fiddle with your phone in the middle of the night. On my phone, I have the AP News notifications turned on so that I might stay informed about the issues that concern me most. As the news and notifications about the news are apathetic and ignorant to the clock, news can break at any hour. Sometimes that news breaks, and we are some of the first to witness emotional responses to the circumstance. It is harrowing to see an important event play out while your part of the world is asleep. As you witness the event, terrible as it might be, the only appropriate first response is prayer.

> "The Spirit of the Lord is upon me,
>   because he has anointed me
>   to bring good news to the poor.
> He has sent me to proclaim release to the captives
>   and recovery of sight to the blind,
>   to set free those who are oppressed,
> to proclaim the year of the Lord's favor." (Luke 4:18-19)

Great Spirit of God,
As the news breaks this night, it is terrible and horrible and all too familiar. It is heartbreaking to see such tragedy, and I do not understand it. To make sense of it in this moment seems futile. It will take time to both realize and recognize the reasoning for this, if there even is any. Don't shy away from me now, or from the situation that is playing out. Focus your loving kindness on those most affected. Do not forget that they are your people, and you love them. Give me peace too if you have some to spare. I don't know how we will get through this scenario, but I trust in you. That's all I've got. Amen.

A Prayer for When Tragedy Strikes during the Night

Recently a friend recommended to me Garrett M. Graff's 2019 book, *The Only Plane in the Sky: An Oral History of 9/11*, an attempt to bring together (at the time) almost two decades of history on the terror attacks of September 11, 2001, from eyewitness accounts, testimonies, and interviews. It struck me as a profound reminder of how precious life is and how tragedy can strike on a clear Tuesday morning or at any other time, even during the nighttime hours.

Though our prayers may seem impossibly trite at such a moment, the need to pray is all the more pressing.

> "I have said this to you so that in me you may have peace. In the world you face persecution. But take heart: I have conquered the world." (John 16:33)

Dear Lord,

Your heart was the first to break this night.[17] Your heart is big, and it is broken, as ours are too. Kindle in us a sense of peace—we need peace so deeply, so fully right now. As the tragedy continues to unfold, it is apparent that we need you now more than ever. Put all things into subjection under your feet so that the world might be reminded that you have conquered this world already, and rebellion in sin will do no good. Fix this mess. The world feels like it is ending, Lord. Keep people safe, and do not hide your face from this world. Amen.

---

17. This sentiment was best articulated by the Rev. William Sloane Coffin, famed Senior Minister of the Riverside Church in New York City, during his eulogy for his son Alex. Rev. Coffin delivered the remarks ten days after his son's death in a car accident.

A Prayer on the Evening of a Death Anniversary

Death anniversaries are difficult and daunting for many. As the calendar day approaches, we feel that the pain will return with its original power. We fear that we might touch the scarring scab so that it bleeds again. This is most prevalent in quiet moments, moments that often happen in the night-time hours. Our best option is to trust in a God who works outside the realm of calendars and dates but is deeply concerned with how we feel, think, and act in the world.

> Joshua said to them, "Pass on before the ark of the LORD your God into the middle of the Jordan, and each of you take up a stone on his shoulder, according to the number of the tribes of the Israelites, so that this may be a sign among you. When your children ask in time to come, 'What do those stones mean to you?' then you shall tell them that the waters of the Jordan were cut off in front of the ark of the covenant of the LORD. When it crossed over the Jordan, the waters of the Jordan were cut off. So these stones shall be to the Israelites a memorial forever." (Joshua 4:5-7)

Dear God, I give thanks that you remember. You remember your servants here on earth, and you hold close to you those servants now gone from my sight whom I miss terribly. Though I know it isn't possible, I would give anything to peel back the veil to see them. I pray that they are well, safe, and whole in your glory. Knowing that all things return to you, I long for the day when I will be reunited in the fullness of time with all that is good. Thank you for remembering your children. Amen.

PRAYERS INSPIRED BY
HYMNS & SCRIPTURE

A Prayer Based on "A Hymn for Midnight" by Charles Wesley

The Rev. Charles Wesley is widely considered to be one of the greatest hymn writers of the age. Born in 1707 in Epworth, Lincolnshire, in England, he wrote more than 6,000 hymns in his lifetime. In 2023, I had the opportunity to preach at the Old North Church, the last extant church where Charles preached on the North American continent. It was a humbling and awe-inspiring moment for this Wesley nerd. This hymn that Wesley penned speaks to God's care and concern for all of creation at any time of day, including the midnight hour. It has words such as these:

> While midnight shades the earth o'erspread,
> And veil the bosom of the deep,
> Nature reclines her weary head,
> And care respires and sorrows sleep;
> My soul still aims at nobler rest,
> Aspiring to her Savior's breast.

> About midnight Paul and Silas were praying and singing hymns to God, and the prisoners were listening to them. Suddenly there was an earthquake so violent that the foundations of the prison were shaken, and immediately all the doors were opened and everyone's chains were unfastened. (Acts 16:25-26)

God of the midnight hour,
It is late and time is fleeting to get some good rest. Yet your love for me is not fleeting or faint. As the clock ticks further into the night, may the fullness of your promises for us be both complete and established in my life forever. In your loving kindness, may the night turn to day and bring forth new possibilities for your kingdom to come here on earth. Then, at last, may you bring us to that heavenly shore where we may be lost in wonder, love, and praise.[18]

Midnight comes and goes, but your love reigns supreme. Thank you, Lord God. Amen.

A Prayer Based on "Abide with Me"

"Abide with Me" is a famous hymn written by Henry Francis Lyte, an Anglican clergyman who lived in the nineteenth century. It was written as a prayer that God might be present throughout the trials and tribulations of life and into the moments that lead to our death. Thy hymn has lyrics such as these: "Abide with me; fast falls the eventide; The darkness deepens; Lord, with me abide. When other helpers fail and

---

18. Charles Wesley, "Love Divine, All Loves Excelling," 1747.

comforts flee, Help of the helpless, Lord, abide with me."[19]

> As they came near the village to which they were going, he walked ahead as if he were going on. But they urged him strongly, saying, "Stay with us, because it is almost evening and the day is now nearly over." So he went in to stay with them. (Luke 24:28-29)

Abide with me, Lord, as you abide with yourself in the glory of the Trinity. The evening is falling to sleep, and darkness is fast at hand. Don't leave me now. Do not abandon your servant. As others flee, as helpers run far from me, you abide. Abide with me because without you I'm nothing. Abide with me because I can't do this by myself. To abide with you in eventide is to know what it's like to experience pain but still seek resurrection. So resurrect us to life anew when morning comes. I yearn for the dawn but feel you close and near. It will be okay. It will be okay. Amen.

19. Henry Francis Lyte, "Abide with Me," 1861.

A Prayer Based on "All Praise to Thee Our God This Night"

Thomas Ken's *All Praise to Thee Our God This Night* is a classic evening hymn. It paints a picture of a majestic and loving God who is both sovereign yet deeply concerned with the happenings of the world. It offers the nighttime as praise to a living and loving God. This hymn was first published in 1695 and remains a standard for compline, vespers, and evensong services. It is often sung with the tune TALLIS' CANON, also known as EVENING HYMN, which was written from the 1560s.

> All praise to Thee, my God, this night,
> For all the blessings of the light.
> Keep me, O keep me, King of kings,
> Beneath the shelter of Thy wings.

> Unless the LORD builds the house, those who build it labor in vain. Unless the LORD guards the city, the guard keeps watch in vain. It is in vain that you rise up early and go late to rest, eating the bread of anxious toil, for he gives sleep to his beloved. (Psalm 127:1-2)

Dear Lord,
You are quick to provide shelter and blessings to your children. Thank you for the ways you show up for me. As the light turns to darkness, keep me close to your loving kindness and be faithful to your promises to me. As you did for saints of old, assure me

of your unwillingness to give up on me. Do not let go of me now. You deserve all praise and honor this night, Lord Christ. All glory belongs to you now and forevermore. Amen.

A Prayer Based on "Phos Hilaron"

Phos Hilaron is one of the oldest hymns of the Christian church beyond those that were recorded in Scripture. The hymn dates to the late third or early fourth century. It translates into English as "O Gladsome Light." It is often used in chants or other forms of music during traditional services of evensong or evening prayer. The hymn is translated from the Greek to read:

> O gracious Light, pure brightness of the ever-living Father in heaven, O Jesus Christ, holy and blessed!
>
> Now as we come to the setting of the sun, and our eyes behold the vesper light, we sing thy praises, O God: Father, Son, and Holy Spirit.
>
> You are worthy at all times to be praised by happy voices, O Son of God, O Giver of life, and to be glorified through all the worlds.

If I say, "Surely the darkness shall cover me,
    and night wraps itself around me,"
even the darkness is not dark to you;
    the night is as bright as the day,
    for darkness is as light to you. (Psalm
    139:11-12)

God of light and darkness, day and night,
As night falls fast upon us in these moments of twilight and evening darkness, help us to see your face—for it is as bright as the sun. You are here with us though we are in the darkness. You are here with us as the light fades. Keep us safe and close at hand. You are worthy of both our praise and adoration, our worship and honor. As your Son, our Savior Jesus Christ, gave us both possibility and promise of life abundant, give us rest this night so that we might live into that abundance in the here and now. We are grateful, and we are in awe of your light. Amen.

A Prayer Based on "Silent Night"

"Stille Nacht" is a timeless Christmas carol written in 1818 by Joseph Mohr in the small hamlet of Oberndorf bei Salzburg in Austria. The song was first offered as a carol at St. Nicholas Parish Church by the young Mohr, a Catholic priest assigned to the parish the year prior.[20] It wasn't even played during the actual service because the organ wasn't working, so the musician was to play on the guitar. Since the church did not approve of guitars for musical worship, it was used after the service. Even still, that Christmas Eve mass, a song was sung that would help shape the course of Christmases to come even to this day: *Silent night, holy night. All is calm, all is bright. Round yon Virgin Mother and Child. Holy infant so tender and mild, sleep in heavenly peace, sleep in heavenly peace.*

> So they went with haste and found Mary and Joseph and the child lying in the manger. When they saw this, they made known what had been told them about this child, and all who heard it were amazed at what the shepherds told them, and Mary treasured all these words and pondered them in her heart. The shepherds returned, glorifying and praising God for all they had heard and seen, just as it had been told them. (Luke 2:16-20)

God the eternal who entered time,
You have the audacity to come at a moment when the empires of the world are crushing down on the lowly and the least. It was scary for Mary and Joseph then, and it is scary for us now to see the world being tossed around by conquerors and oppressors. On silent nights such as this, help me to always side with the ones on the outskirts of empires, in forgotten towns

---

20. Jason Daley, "A Brief History of Silent Night," *Smithsonian Magazine*. December 2018.

and communities. Help me to see once more your story of coming to be with us so that we might be with you. In the silent moments, keep us held strong in your story. May the silent night give way to the fact that joy has come into the world. I give thanks that from that moment on, joy never left. Now for some of that sleep in heavenly peace. Amen.

A Prayer Based on Abram's Covenant with God (Genesis 15:12-21)

Prayer is never prayed in a vacuum. This prayer was written after a text exchange with a friend who was experiencing the pain and heartache of a miscarriage. Her pain was palpable in the conversation. The nights felt so lonely for her, and she sometimes didn't know where to turn. Even still, my confidence in God's compassion for the situation was solidified by my friend's grace, determination, and resiliency. Prayer is never prayed in a vacuum.

> As the sun was going down, a deep sleep fell upon Abram, and a deep and terrifying darkness descended upon him. Then the LORD said to Abram, "Know this for certain, that your offspring shall be aliens in a land that is not theirs and shall

be slaves there, and they shall be oppressed for four hundred years, but I will bring judgment on the nation that they serve, and afterward they shall come out with great possessions. As for yourself, you shall go to your ancestors in peace; you shall be buried in a good old age. And they shall come back here in the fourth generation, for the iniquity of the Amorites is not yet complete."

When the sun had gone down and it was dark, a smoking fire pot and a flaming torch passed between these pieces. On that day the LORD made a covenant with Abram, saying, "To your descendants I give this land, from the river of Egypt to the great river, the River Euphrates, the land of the Kenites, the Kenizzites, the Kadmonites, the Hittites, the Perizzites, the Rephaim, the Amorites, the Canaanites, the Girgashites, and the Jebusites" (Gen 15:12-21).

Covenanting God,
Though often we are shortsighted, you never fall short of your covenant with us. As our lives are littered with anniversaries of what could have been, of what should have been, the assurance of your salvation for us stands firm and supreme. As we mourn the loss of the plans laid that are not coming to fruition help us to see the land you promised for us. Our hope and confidence are in you—and magnified by your great love that has been for us since before we were born. This indeed will lead us to the land beyond the Jordan, and into your embrace. Keep us on track until then. Amen.

A Prayer Based on Jacob Wrestling at Peniel (Genesis 32:22-32)

The story of Jacob wrestling with the heavenly figure at Peniel is one of mystery and beauty. It's truly one of the best narratives that Scripture has to offer. Jacob's estranged brother Esau is close at hand, and because of Jacob's prior actions he believes his brother intends to destroy him. As night falls, Jacob sends his family and earthly treasure across the river and camps at Peniel. There he wrestles with a figure that some attribute to be an angel, while others attribute it to be the very God who has led Jacob thus far. They wrestle all night, and as day breaks and the figure attempts to evade sunrise, Jacob overtakes the being and demands a blessing. The being blesses Jacob and gives him a new name, a name that will bless the world: Israel.

> The same night he got up and took his two wives, his two maids, and his eleven children and crossed the ford of the Jabbok. He took them and sent them across the stream, and likewise everything that he had. Jacob was left alone, and a man wrestled with him until daybreak. When the man saw that he did not prevail against Jacob, he struck him on the hip socket, and Jacob's hip was put out of joint as he wrestled with him. Then he said, "Let me go, for the day is breaking." But

Jacob said, "I will not let you go, unless you bless me." So he said to him, "What is your name?" And he said, "Jacob." Then the man said, "You shall no longer be called Jacob, but Israel, for you have striven with God and with humans and have prevailed." Then Jacob asked him, "Please tell me your name." But he said, "Why is it that you ask my name?" And there he blessed him. So Jacob called the place Peniel, saying, "For I have seen God face to face, yet my life is preserved." The sun rose upon him as he passed Penuel, limping because of his hip. Therefore to this day the Israelites do not eat the thigh muscle that is on the hip socket, because he struck Jacob on the hip socket at the thigh muscle. (Genesis 32:22-32)

God who wrestles with us,
You call me by my name—what a gift that is. Sometimes I take it for granted, and sometimes I ought to listen better. Help me to wrestle more with your calling on my life this night. As I go through nights of fighting and fidgeting, others' perception of me, and even you, Lord God, help me to be worthy of the match. And when my time is at hand, do not withhold your blessing from me. Get me through the night, God. Amen.

A Prayer Based on Jacob's Dream at Bethel (Genesis 28:10-22)

One of the most prolific stories of nighttime comes from the Hebrew Bible and Jacob's journey towards wholeness. As Jacob dreams, he sees visions of angels descending and ascending a ladder. This text has been portrayed in the African American slave spiritual "We Are Climbing Jacob's Ladder." This dream is a sign and seal of God's presence, promise, and providence. God has not abandoned the world to its own devices. God is actively sending angels to take charge and watch over those whom God loves. God does not desert those whom God called to be God's people.

> When he reached a certain place, he stopped for the night because the sun had set. Taking one of the stones there, he put it under his head and lay down to sleep. He had a dream in which he saw a stairway resting on the earth, with its top reaching to heaven, and the angels of God were ascending and descending on it. There above it stood the LORD, and he said: "I am the LORD, the God of your father Abraham and the God of Isaac. I will give you and your descendants the land on which you are lying. Your descendants will be like the dust of the earth, and you will spread out to the west and to the east, to the north and to the south. All peoples on earth will be blessed through you and your offspring. I am with you and will watch over you wherever you go, and I

will bring you back to this land. I will not leave you until I have done what I have promised you."

When Jacob awoke from his sleep, he thought, "Surely the LORD is in this place, and I was not aware of it." He was afraid and said, "How awesome is this place! This is none other than the house of God; this is the gate of heaven." (Genesis 28:10-16 abbreviated)

God of angel armies,

All this talk of angels, spirits, and such gives me pause. I want to believe they would show up if I needed them, yet this world feels incredibly lonely—especially this night. Yet even so, I know that if others cried for help, I would show up for them, and perhaps in that fashion I become the agent of your glory. Help me to climb Jacob's ladder high enough to see who is in need, and then send me there. Truly, you have left the followers of your Son as the revelation of your goodness. May we be worthy of the mantle you have laid upon us. Amen.

PS—We would welcome real angels too.

A Prayer Based on John 1:5

Some of the most powerful lines in John's Gospel are found at the beginning. John's Gospel is clear on the identity of Jesus of Nazareth and seeks to describe him as he is: the Son of the Most High God. John reminds us that God is with us through the gift of God's Son in ways we had not thought possible. This verse shows us that even in the dark places we thought were empty and barren, God is up to something.

> The light shines in the darkness, and the darkness did not overtake it. (John 1:5)

Lord of the Light,
This night the darkness is closing in around me. Tell me again the story of your love for me and how it will never stop or fade. As the light shines through the broken pieces of my existence, I see why you are so crafty and wise. The light is shining through to show that beautiful things can be made from despair. As your Son once graced this world, so too, send your Spirit so that all might come to know your saving love. This I ask in the name of the flame of your Spirit. Amen.

A Prayer Based on John 3

A Pharisee and a Messiah encounter one another in the middle of the night, and we gain one of the most profound lines of Scripture known the world over. John 3:16 unequivocally ranks at the top of most well-known verses: "For God so loved the world that he gave his only begotten son, that whosoever believes in him shall not perish but have everlasting life." It's plastered on poster board at sporting events and often quoted by celebrities. Yet the subsequent verse, verse 17, holds just as much weight—even if it is less familiar: "For God did not send his son into the world to condemn the world, but that the world might be saved through him." Scripture is a profound guide to an abundant life. These verses seem to be the linchpin of it all.

> And just as Moses lifted up the serpent in the wilderness, so must the Son of Man be lifted up, that whoever believes in him may have eternal life. (John 3:14-15)

God who so loved,
You still love me. You loved me enough that you became like me to get to know the human condition, to understand what it meant to be in this world. The world is hard and cold, but you are good. Be kind to me if I come to you in the middle of the night as Nicodemus did, for the world is skeptical and unkind. Yet even still, in my encounter with you, help me to be forever changed as Nicodemus was. Don't let me return the way I came. How sad that would be.

You loved the world. May the world respond in kind. Amen.

A Prayer Based on Psalm 4:8

This book, like many of my books, has taken different forms as it was crafted into what you now hold in your hands. As I added passages of Scripture, I kept returning to the book of Psalms and finding so much that I had either forgotten or missed the last time I studied the book. It is literally our first hymnal, a songbook of experiences and realities faced by prominent and no-name Israelites. The verse before us tonight assures of us God's presence, promise, and protection. It is meaningful and worthwhile to commit it to our memories so that we might know what God intends for us. We are safe in the arms of God.

> I will both lie down and sleep in peace, for you alone, O LORD, make me lie down in safety. (Psalm 4:8)

God of the raging deep and brewing storm,
This night I feel your protection and care. The thunder may be rolling, and the lightning may be flashing across the sky, but I know that I am safe in your watch-care. The pains of life may cut deep, but your promise to me is that under your wing I am secure. May the winds that beat against my life not

destroy, but may my foundation on the Rock of Ages hold fast my whole life long. Amen, and amen.

PRAYERS FOR SPECIAL NIGHTS

A Prayer for the Eve of Epiphany

Epiphany is a feast day in the church that marks the coming of the Magi to the Christ Child after his birth in Bethlehem of Judah. In the Gregorian calendar, it is marked on January 6, twelve days after Christmas (yes, that's where we get the song). The Magi—traditionally named Melchior, Caspar, and Balthazar—brought gifts of gold, frankincense, and myrrh. They did so after seeing the Christ Child's star rise and following it to the place where Jesus was.

> When they saw that the star had stopped, they were overwhelmed with joy. On entering the house, they saw the child with Mary his mother, and they knelt down and paid him homage. Then, opening their treasure chests, they offered him gifts of gold, frankincense, and myrrh. And having been warned in a dream not to return to Herod, they left for their own country by another road. (Matthew 2:10-12)

God of another road,
Nighttime feels like another road. It feels distant from normal and far from what is intended for me. Yet it is on this other road that I see the stars clearer; I see your star in a new and different way. What might your will be for me on this other road? What might your purpose be for sending me this way? Don't forsake your servant now, as Herod is close at hand. Reach us with your starlight once more. Amen.

A Prayer for Ash Wednesday Night

On the church calendar, Ash Wednesday immediately follows Transfiguration Sunday and precedes the First Sunday in Lent. Lent is a season of self-denial, examination, and contrition for our sins. It is a forty-day period (not counting Sundays) before Easter of fasting and prayer. Ash Wednesday stands as the gateway to that forty-day period. As part of the day, ashes are imposed upon the foreheads of faithful Christians throughout the world as a reminder of mortality and the need for repentance and atonement.

> Yet even now, says the LORD, return to me with all your heart, with fasting, with weeping, and with mourning; rend your hearts and not your clothing. Return to the LORD your God, for he is gracious and merciful, slow to anger, abounding in steadfast love, and relenting from punishment. (Joel 2:12-13)

Steadfast Lord,
Your love endures forever. On this night as I think of my own mortality and the consequences of sin, I hope that I might be able to find anew your plan for my life. As these ashes rest on my forehead, may I soon find rest this night. Then, in your goodness, bring me home at last to that heavenly country where

rest is abundant. Holy Lord, I am so thankful for your love. Amen.

A Prayer for Palm Sunday Night

Palm Sunday marks the beginning of the Christian observance of Holy Week, the holiest time of the church year where the faithful remember Christ's triumphant entry into Jerusalem and subsequent passion and death played out over the course of the week. The story of Palm Sunday is one of exuberant exultation and belief that the Messiah had arrived to take back the holy city of Jerusalem. And then Jesus entered the city on a donkey—hardly the entrance of military might. Yet this statement is clear: Jesus is Lord and Caesar is not.

> When he had come near Bethphage and Bethany, at the place called the Mount of Olives, he sent two of the disciples, saying, "Go into the village ahead of you, and as you enter it you will find tied there a colt that has never been ridden. Untie it and bring it here. If anyone asks you, 'Why are you untying it?' just say this, 'The Lord needs it.'" So those who were sent departed and found it as he had told them. As they were untying the colt, its owners asked them, "Why are you untying the colt?" They said, "The Lord needs it." Then they brought it to Jesus, and after throwing their

cloaks on the colt, they set Jesus on it. As he rode along, people kept spreading their cloaks on the road. Now as he was approaching the path down from the Mount of Olives, the whole multitude of the disciples began to praise God joyfully with a loud voice for all the deeds of power that they had seen, saying, "Blessed is the king who comes in the name of the Lord! Peace in heaven, and glory in the highest heaven!" (Luke 19:29-38)

Strong and merciful God,
In our quest for power, we often miss that your Son came to be our Savior not with military might and conquest but as the Prince of Peace. This evening as I reflect on the first Palm Sunday, I know that Jesus must have been so disappointed in humankind's response to his entry into Jerusalem all those years ago. Yet even in his disappointment he did not shy away from his mission. Blessed is the One who comes in the name of the Lord. Hosanna in the highest.

Whether I'm ready or not, holy week is here, dear Lord. Make my heart ready. Amen.

A Prayer for Spy Wednesday Night (Holy Wednesday)

Spy Wednesday, or Holy Wednesday, is the commemoration of Judas's betrayal of Jesus to the Sanhedrin, which led to the Roman authorities crucifying Jesus. This night, we mark the worst possible outcome of God's plan for salvation. All hope seems to dim with the daylight, and we need prayer now more than ever. *The Methodist Book of Worship for Church and Home* from 1965 offers these words: "Assist us mercifully with thy help, O Lord God our salvation, that we may enter with joy upon the meditation of those mighty acts through which thou hast given unto us life and immortality; through Jesus Christ our Lord. Amen."

> Then Judas Iscariot, who was one of the twelve, went to the chief priests in order to betray him to them. When they heard it, they were greatly pleased and promised to give him money. So he began to look for an opportunity to betray him. (Mark 14:10-11)

Lord Jesus,
You have known the pain of betrayal that was of the worst kind. It was both painful and riddled with arrogance, greed, and sadness. "Sometimes it causes me to tremble," the old hymn goes. Sadly, this will only get worse from here, yet I stand firm in your promise that you will make a way out of no way. Tonight, in these moments when we see your betrayal, may we be reminded of the ways we have betrayed you and those around us through our action and through our inaction. Help us to seek new beginnings and look for the dawn that is to come. Amen.

A Prayer for Maundy Thursday Night

The story of Maundy Thursday plays out over the course of a night. It is the night during Holy Week when Jesus celebrated the Passover with his disciples for the last time. This is also the night when Christians believe Jesus instituted the celebration of Holy Communion by saying that the meal they shared was his body and blood. Since then, Christians throughout the ages have celebrated the Eucharist as a means for remembering Christ's sacrifice for us and God's great love God for us.

> For I received from the Lord what I also handed on to you, that the Lord Jesus on the night when he was betrayed took a loaf of bread, and when he had given thanks, he broke it and said, "This is my body that is for you. Do this in remembrance of me." In the same way he took the cup also, after supper, saying, "This cup is the new covenant in my blood. Do this, as often as you drink it, in remembrance of me." For as often as you eat this bread and drink the cup, you proclaim the Lord's death until he comes. (1 Corinthians 11:23-26)

God of love and God of power,
Your infinite love for me is laid bare this night. You have shown me your heart, and your heart is big and wide. It is meant for all of us too. This night you go from dining with your friends to showing us what love looks like as sacrifice. As I witness this transition and this sorrow come to pass, do not allow me to shy away from the moment. May I hold my gaze on you as I lie down to rest. May you be my waking thought as well. This difficult night is not ideal, but Lord, make it part of your plan to bless the world. Amen.

A Prayer for Good Friday Night

The Friday before Easter is part of the Triduum commemoration of Christ's Passover for us, known as Good Friday. But there is hardly anything good about it. This consequential moment in human history plays witness to humanity's attempts to kill the One who gave us life and purpose. We see Jesus mangled and beaten on a cross of wood as the Roman Empire's soldiers jeer and sneer at him. This is the sadness the earth cannot handle. We have killed God.

> Meanwhile, standing near the cross of Jesus were his mother, and his mother's sister, Mary the wife of Clopas, and Mary Magdalene. When Jesus saw his mother and the disciple whom he

loved standing beside her, he said to his mother, "Woman, here is your son." Then he said to the disciple, "Here is your mother." And from that hour the disciple took her into his own home.

After this, when Jesus knew that all was now finished, he said (in order to fulfill the scripture), "I am thirsty." A jar full of sour wine was standing there. So they put a sponge full of the wine on a branch of hyssop and held it to his mouth. When Jesus had received the wine, he said, "It is finished." Then he bowed his head and gave up his spirit. (John 19:25-30)

Jesus,
You know what it's like to die.

That is enough, and yet knowing we did it to you pains me greatly. This night, as the world sits still and sad, I don't really know what to say or how to respond to such a tragic set of circumstances. I'm skeptical to ask for help because you have so much going on, but if you have any guidance or wisdom, do not hold back. Even now as earth awaits what might be next, I feel that you cannot be kept down by what we did. For now, though, we learn to live alone in the world. I hope you hear me; I hope you can help me. Amen.

A Prayer for the Great Vigil of Easter

The Great Vigil of Easter is the first service of the Great Fifty Days of Easter. It's an ancient festival in which, through vigil and prayer, we mark the passing away of Lent and the passing over of our Lord. This was a time when converts to the faith and those who had been removed from the community for their sins were grafted back into the community of the faith through baptism. Through lighting candles, reading lessons, and hearing the proclamation of Easter, we celebrate the first fruits of the resurrection.

Early on the first day of the week, while it was still dark, Mary Magdalene came to the tomb and saw that the stone had been removed from the tomb. So she ran and went to Simon Peter and the other disciple, the one whom Jesus loved, and said to them, "They have taken the Lord out of the tomb, and we do not know where they have laid him." Then Peter and the other disciple set out and went toward the tomb. The two were running together, but the other disciple outran Peter and reached the tomb first. He bent down to look in and saw the linen wrappings lying there, but he did not go in. Then Simon Peter came, following him, and went into the tomb. He saw the linen wrappings lying there, and the cloth that had been on Jesus's head, not lying with the linen wrappings but rolled up in a place by itself. Then the other disciple, who reached the tomb first, also went in, and he saw and believed, for as yet they did not understand the scripture, that he must rise from the dead. Then the disciples returned to their homes. (John 20:1-10)

Risen and Living Christ,
On this most holy night, you became for us the Passover Lamb. You are risen with healing in your wings. Help us to be mindful that this gift you offer us by the glory of your resurrection is meant for all. I am thankful that in the fullness of this night, your abundance overcame the grave. How beautiful it is to lean into that promise. You are alive, and alive forevermore. Help me to sleep this night because there is celebrating to do in the morning. Amen.

A Prayer for Easter Eve

Easter Eve is often a quiet affair, without much pomp and circumstance. Compared to the first Easter Eve, it has always been tame. Journey there in your mind's eye: The Lord is discovered to be risen, and people are confused. Cleopas and his companion are on the road to Emmaus discussing the day's events. A sojourner comes alongside them and reminds them of their sacred story. By the time they reach their resting space that night, they come to the amazing realization that Jesus had been their fellow journeyer all along. The risen Lord was in their midst. Christ the Lord is risen; the Lord is risen indeed!

> They said to each other, "Were not our hearts burning within us while he was talking to us on the road, while he was opening the scriptures to us?" That same hour they got up and returned to Jerusalem, and they found the eleven and their companions gathered together. They were saying, "The Lord has risen indeed, and he has appeared to Simon!" Then they told what had happened on the road and how he had been made known to them in the breaking of the bread. –(Luke 24:31-35)

Lord of life and resurrection,
You make yourself known in the breaking of bread and the sharing of a cup—simple gifts that I often take for granted. In this season of life and newness, don't let it be lost on me that this morning you accomplished everything. This night as I reflect on the beauty of all that you did, I can't help but smile because I know you are alive forevermore. Not only that, but you offer the same gift me, to all. Thank you for the promise that my being will share your same fate. May the resurrection renew and revive this fallow ground. Now grant me holy rest, as there is work to be done to tell this old, old story. Amen.

A Prayer for the Eve of Pentecost

Pentecost marks the coming of the Holy Spirit upon the Apostles who were gathered in a locked room in Jerusalem. Suddenly tongues of fire fell upon them, and they were speaking in various languages. Some of the residents of Jerusalem felt that they were drunk or insane. But this moment was an unleashing of God's Spirit upon the world. We are benefactors of that blessing to this day.

> When the day of Pentecost had come, they were all together in one place. And suddenly from heaven there came a sound like the rush of a violent wind, and it filled the entire house where they were sitting. Divided tongues, as of fire, appeared among them, and a tongue rested on each of them. All of them were filled with the Holy Spirit and began to speak in other languages, as the Spirit gave them ability. (Acts 2:1-4)

Spirit of the Living God,
Something is afoot this night—something is brewing. Help me to be the midwife to your promised presence. Enable me to see the signs that you are here and among us. God, as you plead for the sake of your children, help me also to minister to those who come to mind this night. As Pentecost approaches, I ask that you might do it again. Revive us again. I beg you to give us a double portion of Pentecost for the sake of a hurting world that needs you now. Rain down your fire from the place where you reign. Amen.

A Prayer for Halloween Night

All Hallows' Eve, All Saints' Eve, or, as it is commonly known, Halloween is a celebration marked yearly on October 31, immediately preceding All Saints' Day. It begins the liturgical period of Allsaintstide, which is a period of the liturgical year remembering saints, martyrs, and all those who have departed this life for the life to come. The holiday has roots in Celtic and Gaelic harvest festivals, but today it stands as a fun festival for children to dress up and receive candy as they trick-or-treat. Even still, Halloween remains an important part of the Christian liturgical calendar.

> For to this end Christ died and lived again, so that he might be Lord of both the dead and the living. (Romans 14:9)

Lord of all things,
You have power over the principalities and powers of this world. You subdued the darkness and evil so that we might flourish. Tonight, as our world marks Halloween, keep me mindful that no ghost, ghoul, or goblin can hold any power over the Potentate of Time. May children have fun, and may candy be given, but remind us that the purpose of this night is to signal to the world it has no sway in the kingdom of God. Thanks be to you, Holy One. Amen.

A Prayer to Remember a Saint (All Saints' Day Evening)

All Saints' Day is a holy day in the Christian tradition celebrated on November 1 (with All Saints' Sunday celebrated the Sunday immediately following that date). It has roots in some of the oldest and holiest moments of church history. The day celebrates the acts and works of the saints in High Church traditions, while the Broad Church tradition expands that working definition to include all those now gone from this world and into the world to come.[21]

> After this I looked, and there was a great multitude that no one could count, from every nation, from all tribes and peoples and languages, standing before the throne and before the Lamb, robed in white, with palm branches in their hands. They cried out in a loud voice, saying, "Salvation belongs to our God who is seated on the throne, and to the Lamb!" (Revelation 7:9-10)

God of St. Peter and St. Paul, God of St. Teresa of Calcutta and St. Catherine of Siena, God of my life and witness,

---

21. For the purposes of this book, I will use the expanded definition.

All that comes of our work belongs to you, and all our witness in the world is for your glory. This night I offer special intentions for those whom I love but no longer see here on this earth. I pray especially for [name of departed saints]. As they stand closer to your throne than I, may they pray on my behalf as I pray for them. May you peel back the veil so that I may feel their presence as much as I feel yours. Reassure me of the fullness of your promise so that I might be raised to life when you return for your children. All this I ask in your holy son's name. Amen.

A Prayer for Election Night

The United States of America deems that Federal Elections shall occur "The Tuesday next after the 1st Monday in November, in every even numbered year."[22] Election Night is fraught with emotion for many as returns are rendered by the news media. Many gather around televisions or stare at their phones to watch the results pour in. There will always be disappointed people this night, yet the important reality is that a nation might come together to bind

---

22. "2 U.S. Code § 7—Time of election," *Legal Information Institute*, Cornell Law School, www.law.cornell.edu/uscode/text/2/7.

up their wounds[23] from the previous election cycle. We have so much work to do.

> First of all, then, I urge that supplications, prayers, intercessions, and thanksgivings be made for everyone, for kings and all who are in high positions, so that we may lead a quiet and peaceable life in all godliness and dignity. This is right and acceptable before God our Savior, who desires everyone to be saved and to come to the knowledge of the truth. (1 Timothy 2:1-4)

Dear God,

Save us from our warring madness this night. Do not allow divisions to define our country, our liberty, and our purpose in you. God, you know not political parties, but we follow you under one banner. Help us remember that amid such turbulence. Whatever happens tonight, whoever might win, may your name be praised. Help us to see the good in it all. And if we fail to see such possibility, give us grace to lose with dignity and mutual understanding. Keep watch over our land this night, that we might find your kingdom without national borders on the Last Day. Amen.

---

23. "Lincoln's Second Inaugural Address," 1865, National Park Service, https://www.nps.gov/linc/learn/historyculture/lincoln-second-inaugural.htm.

A Prayer for Thanksgiving Night

The American Thanksgiving holiday is celebrated the fourth Thursday in November. It commemorates the landing of the Pilgrims in Plymouth, Massachusetts, and their first harvest in the New World. It is often portrayed inaccurately in relationship to Indigenous populations. Though Thanksgiving holidays have been declared since President George Washington, President Abraham Lincoln was one who declared it as it is celebrated today.

> Make a joyful noise to the LORD, all the earth.
>> Serve the LORD with gladness;
>> come into his presence with singing.
> Know that the LORD is God.
>> It is he who made us, and we are his;
>> we are his people and the sheep of his pasture.
> Enter his gates with thanksgiving
>> and his courts with praise.
>> Give thanks to him; bless his name.
> For the LORD is good;
>> his steadfast love endures forever
>> and his faithfulness to all generations. (Psalm 100)

Great Creator,
You have given us a feast by which we have enjoyed the food and the company. Bless this night as I continue in the frivolity and fun. I give thanks for the rich bounty of this land, and I acknowledge this night the ways that many have oppressed a few to take custody

of this place. Help me be mindful of those hurting tonight for all the ways that the harm persists. Even still, call me to be mindful of those without homes or families to gather with. In the fullness of this night, remind me that there are those who are empty. Let that humble me. In thanksgiving, I pray. Amen.

A Prayer for Christmas Eve

Christmas Eve is a holy night celebrated each year on December 24. It marks the night in which Christians remember how God became incarnate in the Christ Child. This gift brings forth the beauty of salvation into humankind's realm. While tonight is incredibly holy, it can feel incredibly lonely. Christmas Eve is about family, friendship, worship, and goodwill. Not everyone has those realities readily present in their lives. Tonight, we keep them close to our hearts as we pray and offer thanksgiving for the gift God gave us that night long ago.

> Joseph also went from the town of Nazareth in Galilee to Judea, to the city of David called Beth-lehem, because he was descended from the house and family of David. He went to be registered with Mary, to whom he was engaged and who was expecting a child. While they were there, the time came for her to deliver her child. And

she gave birth to her firstborn son and wrapped him in bands of cloth and laid him in a manger, because there was no place in the guest room. (Luke 2:4-7)

Christmas God,
The hymn so aptly says that "love came down at Christmas,"[24] and indeed it did. I give you thanks for the ways that Christmas shows up anew and fresh every year. I pray for those this night who feel alone, neglected, or afraid. Help them to feel the warm glow of your incarnate love too. And I dare not ask for too much, O God, but bring peace that you promised. Our world is hurting, and the love we offer seems so trite. Infuse it with the beauty of the manger so that it might overpower the forces that seek to undo us. I give you thanks this night for Christmas. May the promise assured all those years ago become true again this night. Amen.

A Prayer for Christmas Night

Christmas night (December 25) is part of the Feast of the Nativity of our Lord. Yet it is incredibly quieter than the hustle and bustle of the previous Advent Season and Christmas Eve. In these moments, it

---

24. Christina Rossetti, "Love Came Down at Christmas," 1885.

might be easy to get lost in your feelings or feel lonely after everyone has returned home. But this moment is precisely why Christ came: so we might feel the abundance of God's presence.

> In the beginning was the Word, and the Word was with God, and the Word was God. He was in the beginning with God. All things came into being through him, and without him not one thing came into being. What has come into being in him was life, and the life was the light of all people. The light shines in the darkness, and the darkness did not overtake it. And the Word became flesh and lived among us, and we have seen his glory, the glory as of a father's only son, full of grace and truth. (John 1:1-5, 14)

Incarnate Lord, you came to live so that we might live too. In the quiet moments amid the wrapping paper and leftover casserole, help us find the Christ Child again. As the evening turns to night, may your presence that brought you here sustain us. Become incarnate in my heart so that the world might see you in me. After all, Christ was born for this. Christ was born for this.[25] Amen.

---

25. John Mason Neale, "Good Christian Friends Rejoice," 1885.

A Prayer for a Watchnight Service

Watchnight services have a long and distinct history in the Jewish and Christian traditions. It was Moses and the Israelites preparing to leave for their freedom who first inspired such a notion. Moravians would celebrate a Lovefeast on the last night of the year as it passed away. John Wesley attended one. That connection brought the tradition to African Methodists in the United States. There, on New Year's Eve 1862, people gathered on "Freedom's Eve" to "watch" for the hour when President Abraham Lincoln's Emancipation Proclamation would come to bear on a warring nation on January 1, 1863. Since then, watchnight services have been widely celebrated by the African American faith community and beyond.

> You shall observe this as a perpetual ordinance for you and your children. When you come to the land that the LORD will give you, as he has promised, you shall keep this observance. And when your children ask you, "What does this observance mean to you?" you shall say, "It is the Passover sacrifice to the LORD, for he passed over the houses of the Israelites in Egypt when he struck down the Egyptians but spared our houses." And the people bowed down and worshiped. The Israelites went and did just as the LORD had commanded Moses and Aaron; so they did. (Exodus 12:24-28)

Liberating and life-giving God,
You freed your people many times from the bondage that kept them bogged down. In your loving fashion, you grafted peoples and communities into your story so that we all might be free. Liberate this world tonight, God. Many of us feel trapped, alone, and bound to the ways this world dispenses glory, wealth, and honor to the undeserving. In your Spirit's kindness, draw near to me and to all the world. Bring us to the land that you promise. Even if we have to leave tonight, make us ready, Holy One. We ask this in the name of Jesus, our Passover Lamb. Amen.

A Prayer for New Year's Eve

December 31 marks the end of the Gregorian calendar year, and thus New Year's Eve is a time of celebration, reflection, and expectation. This night, of all the nights, is often celebrated with those most dear to us. It is both exciting and daunting to consider the passage of time. Poets have mused countless lines about what it means to experience such passage, and hymnists and songwriters have spilled gallons of ink creating a vast musicscape for the experience of time. This night is an opportunity to remain resolved that though the passage of time is certain, people can face it with frivolity and fun. This is our journey.

But do not ignore this one fact, beloved, that with the Lord one day is like a thousand years, and a thousand years are like one day. The Lord is not slow about his promise, as some think of slowness, but is patient with you, not wanting any to perish but all to come to repentance. But the day of the Lord will come like a thief, and then the heavens will pass away with a loud noise, and the elements will be destroyed with fire, and the earth and everything that is done on it will be disclosed. (2 Peter 3:8-10)

Potentate of Time,
Time is both friend and foe, enemy and compatriot. Bless the time I've been given and will be given in this life so that it might be for your glory and my sanctification. In your charity, remember me as I fear what the future holds this night. With each passing year, the world seems all the more broken. Help us to fix this mess, Lord, even as we count down:

10
9
8
7
6
5
4
3
2
1

May God lift up God's countenance and offer blessings upon us in the year ahead. Amen.

CONCLUSION AND BENEDICTION

Any good book, like nighttime, must have a conclusion. Endless nighttime would not be fun or ideal. Perhaps the gifts of realities like nighttime and daytime is that they pose opportunities for respite from each other. Without night we would grow bored and tired of daytime, and without night we would not be able to take rest from the busyness of day. They each feed off one another, they are symbiotic, and they are part of God's intent for the world. I hope your perception of nighttime shifted as you read the prayers in this book. I hope you find that the time defined within the confines of night is more beautiful than before. God's grace abounds in the night.

When I was in my first year of undergraduate studies at Appalachian State University, that December right before exams, a group of us drove out to Price Lake, a lake on the Blue Ridge Parkway on the outskirts of the mountain town of Boone. As the lights of the small bucolic town faded into the rearview mirror, it was as if the sky were ripped open to reveal a multitude of stars, the likes of which I had not seen before. We all marveled at the majesty of the moment, at how transcendent it was. Though I have lost touch with those people, that memory remains at the top among all my college memories. As life comes into focus, I realize now that moment would not have been possible in the daytime or even in the town limits with its light pollution. The only way this moment of beauty was possible was because I was willing to follow the road deep into darkness and find God there.

It's easy to romanticize the dark at times like that, as I have just done. To be clear, darkness is rowdy; it is disorienting and disillusioning. But God is in the dark just as God is in the day. In fact, I believe that's where God does some of God's best work. God does not disappoint in moments when it is darkest. God shows up and reveals the stars.

In John 3, one of the most prolific and well-known stories of Scripture plays out. Nicodemus, a member of the Sanhedrin, comes to Jesus under the cover of night. While some scholars suggest that this Pharisee was only casually inquisitive, to me his visit paints a vivid picture of yearning to know more despite the perceived trappings of one's own viewpoint. Nicodemus wanted to know if he could take Jesus for his word, and he could only assess this alone and unincumbered by those who had their misgivings and doubts.

Later in John's Gospel, we again find ourselves around a dinner table at nighttime. Reclining with his friends, Jesus showed them what it meant to call someone a friend and told them that the forces of wickedness are great, but the grace of God is greater. Nighttime is a gift from God. The night offers rejuvenation and revitalization. It can lead to clarity and possibility; it can be the assurance that God makes all things new. This prayerbook serves as a testament to the goodness of God. It shows that the nighttime is both beautiful and challenging, but God's grace is sure amid it all. I hope the prayers you lift and offer for yourself from the book shape you and form your response to the darkness. I hope you are both filled and sustained when the going gets tough or when the joy is overwhelming. These are the gifts of God for the people of God. The only faithful response God's people can have as an answer to those gifts is, "Thanks be to God."

A Benediction

Everything that begins must find its completion. Every start has a finish, and every new thing one day grows to an end. Thus, this book ends its liturgical portion with a blessing, a benediction by which your joy may be found complete on the Day of the Lord. Offer this benediction as a prayer of thanksgiving and supplication for the ways that nighttime intersects with our existence.

I am confident of this, that the one who began a good work in you will continue to complete it until the day of Jesus Christ. (Philippians 1:6)

May you have nights that bring you to tears with laughter and joy with those you love most.
May you have nights when you look up and see the stars.
May you have nights that you wish would never end.
May you feel God so near at nighttime that your days become more bearable and brighter.
May the moon shine bright in such a way that you have clarity of purpose and willpower.

Lord, bless those who feel alone.
Bless those who feel without purpose.
Bless those who need your healing touch this night.
Bless those who are frightened or estranged from those they love.
Bless the dying and those in the most pain.

Keep those we love safe, Lord, and may they sleep in peace knowing they are surrounded by love. And when our days are accomplished, bring us at last to that heavenly country where night is a part of history. This blessing is offered in the name of the one in whom darkness is not known and nighttime flees. Amen.

About the Author

The Rev. Dr. Robert W. Lee is a pastor, public theologian, and author. He is a graduate of Appalachian State University (BA), Duke University Divinity School (MTS), and Pacific School of Religion (DMin). He was an endowed scholar while at Duke and graduated with honors from Pacific School of Religion. Lee rose to national prominence in 2017 when he appeared on the *MTV Video Music Awards* and ABC's *The View* in response to the violence in Charlottesville, Virginia, by white supremacists. Dr. Lee spoke out about the need to remove the statues of his collateral ancestor, Confederate General Robert E. Lee. He participated in national negotiations and the conversation surrounding Confederate monuments, including testifying before the United States Congress in July 2020. He participated in the Inaugural Prayer Service for President Joseph R. Biden Jr. in January 2021. In addition to his public theology work, he has served small, middle-sized, and large churches over his career.

Dr. Lee is a sought-after preacher. He has preached from such pulpits as Boston's Old North Church, Harvard University's Memorial Church, the

University of Chicago's Rockefeller Chapel, Foundry United Methodist Church in Washington DC, the Historic Ebenezer Baptist Church in Atlanta, First Presbyterian Church in Birmingham, and the American Cathedral in Paris. He has lectured at universities and seminaries including Arizona State University, St. Michael's College, Union Presbyterian Seminary in Richmond, Union Theological Seminary in New York City, and Spartanburg Methodist College. In 2022, Morehouse College conferred on him membership in the Board of Preachers in the College of Ministers and Laity for the Morehouse College Chapel.

Rob is the author of four books prior to this one, including *Stained-Glass Millennials* (2017), *A Sin by Any Other Name: Reckoning with Racism and the Heritage of the South* (2019), *The Pulpit and the Paper: A Pastor's Coming of Age in Newsprint* (2020), and *Fostering Hope: A Prayerbook for Foster and Adoptive Families* (2022). He had a newspaper column in the *Statesville Record and Landmark* from 2011 until 2018 and continues to write regularly for various ecclesial and secular outlets. Rob and his wife, Stephanie, are the parents to two daughters, Athena and Phoenix. They have two four-legged children, Frank and Maggie. The Lees live in Statesville, North Carolina. Rob is an avid autograph collector.

www.ingramcontent.com/pod-product-compliance
Lightning Source LLC
Chambersburg PA
CBHW071224090426
42736CB00014B/2964

Advance Praise for *Night Owl Prayers*

Spiritually, what could be more daunting than the things that go bump in the night? What an illuminated idea Rob Lee had to devise prayers for us in those difficult nocturnal hours and moods, and what ingenious execution! *Night Owl Prayers: A Prayerbook* meets a profoundly undealt-with need for people who struggle in the dark, and might (with Lee's able guidance) find comfort and hope in God's presence in their darkest moments. A gift you'll pull out your flashlight to read and pray at 3 a.m.

— *The Rev. Dr. James C. Howell, Senior Pastor*
Myers Park United Methodist Church
Charlotte, North Carolina

For all of us who suffer from insomnia—whether occasional or chronic—*Night Owl Prayers* is a godsend. This collection of brief meditations and honest prayers can help us "sabotage sleeplessness," deriving something good (a heart reaching out to divine love) from something crummy (a night of tossing and turning in bed).

— *Brian D. McLaren*
Author and Public Theologian

The ancient words of St Patrick's Breastplate—Christ be with me, Christ within me, Christ behind me, Christ before me—become flesh in this honest book of ingenuous devotions. Rob Lee invites us all to join him in opening every aspect of our lives to Christ's blessing and transformation.

— *The Rev. Dr. Samuel Wells*
Vicar of St Martin-in-the-Fields
London, England

Smyth & Helwys Publishing, Inc.
6316 Peake Road
Macon, Georgia 31210-3960
1-800-747-3016
©2024 by Robert W. Lee
All rights reserved.

All Scripture quotations are from the New Revised Standard Version (updated edition) of the Bible unless otherwise noted.

Library of Congress Cataloging-in-Publication Data on file